Nationalized Politics

# Nationalized Politics

*Evaluating Electoral Politics across Time*

**JAMIE L. CARSON**

**JOEL SIEVERT**

AND

**RYAN D. WILLIAMSON**

Oxford University Press is a department of the University of Oxford. It furthers
the University's objective of excellence in research, scholarship, and education
by publishing worldwide. Oxford is a registered trade mark of Oxford University
Press in the UK and certain other countries.

Published in the United States of America by Oxford University Press
198 Madison Avenue, New York, NY 10016, United States of America.

© Oxford University Press 2024

All rights reserved. No part of this publication may be reproduced, stored in
a retrieval system, or transmitted, in any form or by any means, without the
prior permission in writing of Oxford University Press, or as expressly permitted
by law, by license, or under terms agreed with the appropriate reproduction
rights organization. Inquiries concerning reproduction outside the scope of the
above should be sent to the Rights Department, Oxford University Press, at the
address above.

You must not circulate this work in any other form
and you must impose this same condition on any acquirer.

CIP data is on file at the Library of Congress

ISBN 978–0–19–766966–2 (pbk.)
ISBN 978–0–19–766965–5 (hbk.)

DOI: 10.1093/oso/9780197669655.001.0001

# CONTENTS

Acknowledgments vii

1. Introduction 1
2. Nationalized Elections: A Review 12
3. Evidence of Nationalization across Time 23
4. Nationalization and the Electoral Connection 41
5. Nationalization and Incumbency 64
6. Nationalization and Polarization 94
7. Nationalization and Candidate Evaluations 114
8. Contextualizing Nationalization: The 2020 Elections 139
9. Conclusion 157

Appendix 165
Notes 167
References 177
Index 191

# ACKNOWLEDGMENTS

Writing a book requires a lot of time and effort that inevitably takes away from other aspects of one's life, and this one was no exception. Despite the amount of time that each of us has committed to this project over the past few years, we believe the end result was definitely worth it. During the past two decades, we have witnessed increasing amounts of nationalized electoral and political behavior in American politics. These changes have yielded several unexpected consequences and led scholars to scratch their heads at such developments. Events during the past decade in particular have led many to question the durability of existing political institutions and the very foundations of American democracy—this was most recently illustrated by the siege of the U.S. Capitol in January 2021 by a group of citizens who remained unconvinced that President Donald Trump had lost the 2020 election via legitimate means. As social scientists, we seek to investigate these types of phenomena in as impartial a manner as possible to better understand both the explanations for and the effects of this increasingly nationalized political environment.

Like many book projects, this manuscript started out as a series of separate but related conference papers that we eventually realized were conveying a similar message about the underlying causes and consequences of nationalization in American politics. We began by seeking to better explain how nationalization across different political eras might help us better evaluate similar trends observed in the incumbency advantage for members of Congress over time. Then we looked at other phenomena, such as polarization levels in Congress, the electoral connection, and evaluations of individual candidates across different eras. In time, we came to the realization that we had more than enough new insights to write what we hope will be an important book about nationalized politics in both the modern and historical eras. Indeed, the culmination of these efforts have resulted in what you are currently holding in your hand.

Each of us owes a debt of gratitude to a number of friends and colleagues who have read various chapters of this book in different forms over nearly the past decade. Although they may not have realized it at the time, their comments were instrumental in taking some of our (very) preliminary ideas and helping us frame them in a more consistent and precise manner. None of them is responsible for any remaining errors that might have made it into the final version of the book, but they definitely prevented us from missing important insights or other valuable interpretations of the data and evidence that we presented over the years.

We presented chapters of this book at several political science conferences over the years, and we want to single out several of our professional colleagues who offered us helpful advice in one form or another. Although we are likely to miss a few individuals along the way, we especially want to thank colleagues at Vanderbilt University who attended the Congress and History meeting in 2015, where we presented an earlier version of Chapter 5. We want to mention the especially helpful comments offered by Richard Bensel, Sarah Binder, Robert Erikson, Jeff Jenkins, Frances Lee, Kenny Lowande, Tim Nokken, Bruce Oppenheimer, Max Palmer, Justin Peck, Steve Smith, and Greg Wawro. We also want to thank the participants who attended and hosted the 2016 Congress and History Conference at the University of Oklahoma, including John Baughman, Mike Crespin, Robert Erikson, Charles Finocchiaro, James Snyder, Charles Stewart III, and Patrick Tucker in reference to Chapter 6. Additionally, we want to thank Justin Buchler for the helpful comments we received at the 2021 MPSA meeting in Chicago on Chapter 4. Finally, we wish to thank Thad Kousser, Paul Musgrave, and Ben Noble for the helpful comments we received on Chapter 7 at the 2022 APSA meeting in Montreal.

# Acknowledgments

Jamie would like to thank his colleagues at the University of Georgia whom he has spoken to about various aspects of his book including Alexa Bankert, Chuck Bullock, George Krause, Michael Lynch, Tony Madonna, Steve Nicholson, Keith Poole, Geoff Sheagley, and Teena Wilhelm. Many of their insights were directly incorporated into the book, and he is truly thankful for the time spent discussing these ideas.

Joel would like to thank his colleagues at Texas Tech University, including Kevin Banda, Seth McKee, Tim Nokken, Ali Stoyan, Frank Thames, and Toby Rider, who all served as sounding boards while he worked on different chapters of the book. Kevin merits special recognition as he offered invaluable advice about the construction of the survey experiment we analyze in Chapter 7. Last, and most important, Joel's professional successes would never have been possible without the love and support from his wife, Kyla Linde, who has made multiple moves across the country so he could pursue his dream career.

Ryan would like to thank his dog, Zuzu, for her loyal companionship and for making him step away from the computer from time to time, thereby helping him preserve his sanity. He was fortunate to have many wells to draw motivation from, and he is thankful to those whose words propelled him forward. He would like to thank his grandfather, who told him he should have been a "real" doctor if he was going to spend so many more years in school; his high school football coach, who told him he was "pissing his life away" when he decided sports were no longer the best use of his time; the anonymous people on the internet who went out of their way to say Ryan was not qualified or worthy of his professorship; and to everyone who ever doubted him, including past versions of himself. All of these people challenged him and pushed him to do everything in his power to succeed—in spite of their words.

On a related point, two of the three authors of this book are especially thankful for coffee, without which this project would likely never have been completed.

We are incredibly grateful to Angela Chnapko, who took interest in our original idea and convinced us to seek out an advance contract from Oxford University Press to publish the book. We also wish to thank the anonymous reviewers at Oxford University Press for their excellent comments and suggestions.

Chapter 5 builds upon and extends prior work by Jamie Carson, Joel Sievert, and Ryan Williamson, 2020, "Nationalization and the Incumbency Advantage," published in *Political Research Quarterly* 73(1): 156–168. We gratefully acknowledge that journal's permission to reuse portions of that earlier work here.

We dedicate this book to Gary Jacobson and Keith Poole, two of the giants in the political science discipline who have had a tremendous influence on each of us in various ways. Without their creativeness, inspiration, and seminal research on Congress, there is a good chance this book might never have been written.

# 1

# Introduction

During the past few decades, elections in the United States have become more focused on national politics at the expense of local or contest-specific issues. One of the first attempts at "nationalizing" elections came in 1994, when Newt Gingrich (R-GA) sought to actively recruit experienced Republican challengers across the country to compete in as many congressional races as possible to maximize the Republicans' chances of winning back control of the House. In conjunction with running on their proposed "Contract with America" that fall, Republican candidates sought to capitalize on the growing unpopularity of incumbent President Bill Clinton, who made several missteps during his first two years in office. Indeed, Republican strategists opted to run campaign ads attacking some of the most vulnerable Democratic incumbents in the fall election by trying to link the Democrats explicitly to President Clinton. What was unique about these ads was the use of new computer technology that allowed them to digitally morph the images of individual incumbents into the face of Clinton, whose overall approval had dipped below 40 percent on multiple occasions.

The Republicans' new campaign strategy was first employed in a May 1994 special election held in Kentucky to fill a vacancy created after Democratic incumbent William Natcher, who had represented the second district since 1953, died in March of that year.[1] Ron Lewis, a former college professor and Baptist minister, emerged to challenge Natcher; many viewed him initially as a "sacrificial lamb" since Democrats had previously

*Nationalized Politics.* Jamie L. Carson, Joel Sievert, and Ryan D. Williamson, Oxford University Press.
© Oxford University Press 2024. DOI: 10.1093/oso/9780197669655.003.0001

controlled the seat since 1865. After Natcher's death, however, Republicans threw their support behind Lewis in the special election against Democratic nominee Joe Prather, a former Kentucky state legislator who sought to win on his own without assistance from the Democratic Party.[2] In a series of ads prior to the special election, Republicans featured the face of Prather morphing into the face of Clinton, with a voice-over stating, "If you like Bill Clinton, you'll love Joe Prather. Kentucky doesn't need another professional politician." Lewis ended up finishing with 55 percent of the vote, compared to 45 percent for Prather.[3]

The triumph of the national over local politics in American elections did not abate as the nation entered the start of a new century. During the 2016 elections, every state won by Hillary Clinton elected a Democratic senator, while every state won by Donald Trump elected a senator from the Republican Party. The strong correspondence between the presidential and senatorial contests led pundits to declare the 2016 Senate elections "the most nationalized ever."[4] In the 2018 Senate and gubernatorial elections, the trend continued as political observers noted that "most voters are casting straight ticket ballots."[5] The 2020 elections continued this trend, as every state except Maine supported co-partisan Senate and presidential candidates. Despite the fact that the overwhelming majority of states do not provide a straight-ticket voting option on the ballot, most voters consistently offer support for only one party's candidates, even without the president on the ballot.[6] These high levels of partisan loyalty are similar to that witnessed by voters casting party ballots during most of the 19th century, when voters often had little or no choice but to cast a straight-ticket vote as a result of the party ballot that was in use at the time.

The greater focus on national political issues is not limited to congressional or gubernatorial elections, however. During the early 2010s, state legislators regularly campaigned for reelection by expressing either their support for or opposition to the Affordable Care Act, often simply referred to as "Obamacare" by Republicans—the healthcare reform legislation passed during President Barack Obama's first term. Although most state legislatures did not have jurisdiction over many of the issues that fell under the purview of the national healthcare legislation, that did not stop state legislative candidates from taking strong stances either in favor of or against this legislation during the campaign season. Indeed, many states introduced legislation that aimed to either prop up or cripple various aspects of the healthcare bill.[7] One of the main reasons state legislators engaged in this behavior is that they recognized the utility in exploiting a highly nationalized and controversial policy that would resonate with their voters on election day based on their expressed support or, more often, opposition.

In recent years, election scholars have studied these developments under the framework of election nationalization. By "nationalization," we are referring to a phenomenon in which top-down forces, such as presidential vote choice or partisanship, inform voters' decisions in subnational elections rather than candidate-specific factors or local forces. In other words, voters have increasingly become less likely to take local or regional factors into account when choosing between different candidates on the ballot and instead base their decisions about who to vote for or engage in political discussions on a broader range of considerations. For instance, voters may select local or statewide candidates based on specific national policies (e.g., the Affordable Care Act or the creation of the Department of Homeland Security after 9/11) or who is currently occupying the White House. More specifically, our definition of nationalization aligns closely with that of Hopkins (2018, 34): "[N]ational and local politics are fought over related dimensions.... [A]s a consequence, national political divisions infuse subnational politics and political engagement is primarily national in orientation." While there are certainly alternative ways to define nationalization, our definition is consistent with other recent studies on nationalization in congressional elections (see, e.g., Abramowitz and Webster 2016; Fiorina 2016; Jacobson 2015a, 2015c; Sievert and McKee 2019).[8]

A key feature that sets our study apart, however, is that we explore the relationship between nationalization and politics across a wider swath of history. Most of the recent work on nationalization, for instance, explores this phenomenon largely in the context of elections held during the past few decades. On one hand, this makes a lot of sense as the increased nationalization observed in recent decades reflects a pattern that is fundamentally different from the conventional wisdom that "all politics is local." Nevertheless, we believe it is important to consider a longer time period when studying nationalized elections, as we and other congressional elections scholars define them, since they are not a new phenomenon. Elections during the mid- to late 19th century, for instance, were widely acknowledged to be more partisan and nationalized affairs (Burnham 1965; Engstrom and Kernell 2005, 2014). Indeed, the candidate at the top of the ticket was generally perceived to influence down-ballot races since voters were not allowed to pick and choose among various offices when voting, as is the case today.

The extent of nationalization has now reached levels unseen since the 19th century, when the party ballot was in use and voters were generally unable to select among individual candidates. There are, of course, important differences between the electoral politics of the 19th century and today. During the 19th century, the strong linkage between presidential and subnational voting, which is a common measure for defining nationalization (Brady, D'Onofrio, and Fiorina 2000; Erikson 2016; Jacobson 2015c), was a result of electoral institutions like the party ballot in use during this period, which forced voters to select among parties rather than candidates for office (Engstrom and Kernell 2005; Engstrom 2012). With the adoption of progressive reforms such as the Australian ballot and the direct primary, elections became far less nationalized throughout the first half of the 20th century, which allowed for an increased role for incumbency and local influences as well as more candidate-centered elections (Carson and Roberts 2013). The resurgence of nationalization during the past few decades, however, is not typically viewed as a function of institutional arrangements, as was once the case, but is attributed to decisions made by and attitudes among individual voters (Abramowitz and Webster 2016; Fiorina 2016; Hopkins 2018; Jacobson 2015c; Sievert and McKee 2019).

These explanatory differences aside, the return of nationalized electoral contests provides a unique opportunity to analyze changes in elections across nearly two centuries of American electoral history. By examining 180 years of elections, our study leverages considerable differences in electoral competition, electoral rules, nationalization, polarization, and partisan advantage via the incumbency advantage. The purpose of this, book, then is to ask and answer the question "How has nationalization influenced elections across different political eras?" That is the overriding goal of this book. Although we are beginning to see the effects of greater nationalization, we still do not have a firm grasp of the factors that may be contributing to nationalization in the modern era, nor do we fully understand its consequences. Are the factors similar to institutional factors that led to more nationalized elections during the past, or are they a function of behavioral differences stemming from political elites or voters? Is it possible for nationalization to have distinct causes in different eras but similar political effects? When, and under what conditions, are the factors contributing to nationalization likely to recede, and what lessons can we draw upon from the past in addressing these issues? These are the types of questions that we seek to systematically explore in the pages that follow.

## WHY STUDY NATIONALIZATION?

As we indicated, politics were highly nationalized during much of the 19th century because of the party ballot in use at the time. When voters went to the polls on election day, they had little choice but to vote a single-party ticket since voting was often done out in the open and any attempts to split one's ticket were met with suspicion or distrust on the part of party officials who often monitored voters' behavior. Although there were certainly exceptions (on this point, see Carson and Sievert 2018), much of electoral politics during this period was driven by the candidates at the top of the ticket. Accordingly, a popular presidential candidate could yield substantial gains for candidates of his party who would "ride his coattails" into office. At the same time, a candidate with significant political baggage could spell disaster during a presidential election or in a midterm.

Following the adoption of the Australian ballot and direct primaries during the Progressive Era, politics became much less nationalized over the ensuing decades. Voters could now regularly split their tickets, and candidates further down the ballot no longer had their electoral fortunes as closely tied to the individual(s) at the top of the ticket. This was the case for several decades, and elections eventually became more candidate-centered as a result. The rise of more candidate-focused electoral politics led to a rise in incumbent reelection rates starting in the 1960s as well as a dramatic increase in candidate spending due to the emphasis on more localized factors in congressional elections. Even presidential candidates ran campaigns that were more regional in nature, as reflected by Nixon's "Southern Strategy," which represented a significant shift from the politics of old. Indeed, Republicans were generally considered to be more successful at winning the White House in this era, while Democrats largely controlled the U.S. Congress, which necessarily required a level of split-ticket voting previously unseen.

Beginning in the 1980s and continuing into the 1990s, we once again witnessed a gradual shift toward more nationalized elections. Congressional candidates running in the 1980s began emphasizing many of the same issues repeated by Presidents Ronald Reagan and George H. W. Bush during their reelection campaigns. As noted at the beginning of the chapter, during the 1994 congressional elections new technology was employed to digitally morph Democratic candidates' faces into that of President Clinton, who was considerably less popular than he had been when elected two years earlier (Jacobson 1996). Although George W. Bush was not on the ballot during the 2006 midterms, Democratic strategists sought to remind voters how closely tied congressional representatives were to him using their party unity scores. A similar strategy was employed by Republicans in the 2010 midterms given the increasing unpopularity of President Obama, which resulted in Democrats losing control of Congress in that election (Jacobson 2011).

The trend continued later in the decade, although in a somewhat different fashion; members of Congress began to try to distance themselves from their own party's leadership to secure their electoral futures. Many Democratic candidates in the 2018 midterm elections strongly emphasized during their campaigns that their first vote in Congress would be against Nancy Pelosi as Speaker of the House of Representatives, instead of placing emphasis on more substantive or district-specific matters.[9] Additionally, sitting members in recent years have found creative ways to distance themselves from their party leaders. For example, some incumbent legislators will vote against approval of the House journal—a constitutionally mandated record of the day's proceedings within the House—which generally does not, or should not, result in a close vote. However, members can use this procedural vote as a mechanism to say they had defied leadership and voted differently from their party. The hope was that by doing so they had insulated themselves from attacks tying them to national political figures.

In each of the elections discussed above, increased nationalization played a significant role in the electoral outcomes. Candidates running for reelection often have their electoral fortunes tied directly to a president—especially at a midterm—but that phenomenon has become even more pronounced during the past few decades. Candidates who could once get reelected by emphasizing local factors like advertising, credit claiming, or constituency service have a much harder time employing such reelection strategies in a more nationalized electoral environment (Kaslovsky 2022). Under those circumstances, candidates who share a party affiliation with the president are more likely to have their behavior scrutinized in connection with the person currently occupying the White House—for better or for worse.

The preceding statements are particularly pertinent when we consider the events leading up to the 2020 presidential election along with all the elections that would occur simultaneously. Although it is not uncommon for House or Senate candidates to express their support for or opposition to the current occupant of the White House, this was taken to an extreme in 2020. In the congressional primaries, for instance, a significant majority of Republican candidates defined their candidacies through their unconditional support of President Trump and his policies. Even though the president saw a modest increase in approval prior to March 2020 before gradually declining again because of the ongoing COVID-19 pandemic, the besieged economy, and significant outrage over racial relations in the United States, many Republicans did not waver in their support of the president. At the same time, Democratic candidates, including presidential nominee and former vice president Joe Biden, took every opportunity to point out how the sitting president was at the center of many of the problems the country was facing. Thus, it was no exaggeration to say that President Trump overshadowed the 2020 elections in every possible way.

In addition to the electoral consequences of Trump's presence in the 2020 elections, the increased level of nationalization also yielded both direct and indirect effects on democratic accountability and representation. When politics was less nationalized, House and Senate candidates could run campaigns independent of the president, unlike elections during the party ballot era. With this new era of nationalization, candidates' electoral fortunes are once again more directly tied to the president, which makes it more difficult for them to get reelected on their own merits. Indeed, some Republican incumbents encouraged voters to not judge their reelection campaigns based on their feelings about President Trump. In an interview with *Roll Call*, Representative Rodney Davis (R-IL) said, "People who don't like the president, they came out in droves in 2018 by voting against me. Last time, we were the only way somebody could voice displeasure with the president. Now, they've got an opportunity to, if they don't like him, they can also balance out their votes."[10] The greater linkage between presidential and congressional candidates has direct effects on the ability to hold elected officials *individually* accountable since such efforts are now being influenced collectively because of the greater nationalization. With figures like former president Trump looming large in political circles, it becomes difficult for congressional candidates to try to distinguish themselves to their voters, thus directly impacting representation.

Since this increased nationalization does not appear to be a function of electoral rules in place—as was once the case—it becomes even more difficult to try to diagnose possible reforms since much of the effect is likely a function of changes in voter behavior over time. In the remainder of the book, we seek to investigate this phenomenon in greater detail so we can better understand both the underlying causes as well as the consequences of nationalization over much of the history of the United States. Indeed, we believe that many of the changes observed in the electorate during the past few decades is partially a function of how both presidential and congressional candidates have chosen to present themselves in their political campaigns.

## SCOPE OF THE BOOK

We examine a variety of puzzles related to nationalization in the political sphere over time. Specifically, the rest of this work proceeds as follows. In Chapter 2, we review the existing literature on the nationalization of elections. Most of the research on this topic has focused on the recent increase in the nationalization of elections. However, as previously mentioned, we demonstrate that this is not the first time in American political history that nationalization has been so prevalent. The institutions in place during the 19th century necessarily induced high levels of partisan loyalty among those voting. We examine much of this historical literature to place our understanding of nationalization in a broader historical context.

In Chapter 3, we compare nationalization between the 19th century and today. Nationalization during the 19th century was an artifact of institutional design—namely the party ballot (Engstrom and Kernell 2014). During this era, voters necessarily offered greater support for the same party in presidential and subnational elections (a common measure of nationalization). By contrast, nationalization today is believed to be a function of voter choice based largely on increased levels of polarization (Abramowitz and Webster 2016; Hopkins 2018; Sievert and McKee 2019). Although the forces that drive nationalization may differ across historical periods, the effects on election outcomes, the incumbency advantage, polarization, and voter behavior vary in predictable ways regardless of the factors producing increased or decreased nationalization.

In Chapter 4, we investigate the relationship between nationalization and the electoral connection. Some works suggest that nationalization has the potential to weaken the relationship between constituents and voters (e.g., Hopkins 2018), while other research reaches a different conclusion.

For example, Carson and Sievert (2018) show that it is possible for congressional candidates to establish an electoral connection with voters even during a highly nationalized era of politics. This is largely a result of the various electoral rules in place at the time that differ from those influencing elections today. Congressional elections were often held on different days from the presidential election throughout much of the 19th century, for instance, which suggests that nationalization would not necessarily be an overriding factor in all elections held during this era (unlike modern elections).

In Chapter 5, we examine the connection between nationalization and incumbency that was first identified by Jacobson (2015b). In his analysis, Jacobson (2015b) attributes the rise and decline of the incumbency advantage in recent decades to variation in the nationalization of congressional elections. Specifically, he focuses on changes in the association between voters' choices in congressional and presidential election and party loyalty among the electorate. Our findings suggest that incumbents have always enjoyed some electoral advantages, but the magnitude of the incumbency advantage fluctuates in predictable ways over time, with changes in both institutional and political conditions (Carson, Sievert, and Williamson 2020).

In Chapter 6, we examine the connection between nationalization and polarization in Congress. This work builds on Hopkins (2018, 6), who argues that though "polarization and legislative gridlock have many causes, nationalized political behavior is an underappreciated one." Specifically, we theorize that in periods of low nationalization, a moderate candidate may be able to attract support from voters of the opposite party to win a seat in Congress. As nationalization increases, however, ideological congruity may fail to lead a candidate to victory if she affiliates with the "wrong" party. By again leveraging immense historical variation, we can offer an alternative explanation for the changing levels of congressional polarization observed during the past 180 years.

Next, we evaluate various behavioral factors that can enhance nationalization in the modern era via survey experiments in Chapter 7. Jacobson (2015c), for instance, maintains that in recent decades voters have become more likely to align their voting behavior across presidential and congressional races. This raises an important question that we intend to explore: Are voters making this choice intentionally, or are they simply responding to the types of nationalized campaigns that candidates are now running (which is more analogous to the conditions present during the 19th century)? We seek to address this question more systematically using experimental evidence in this chapter.

In Chapter 8, we provide a more in-depth analysis of the current nationalized American political environment. Specifically, we examine the 2020 congressional elections and the 2021 gubernatorial elections and how nationalization shaped these outcomes. We pay special attention to how nationalization shapes candidate endorsements in the modern era as well as how it complicates electoral accountability. We conclude with a discussion of what to expect in future elections and provide insights on whether this trend will subside or if it represents a new norm in American politics.

Finally, in Chapter 9, we summarize our key findings and contributions, further discuss the implications of our work for the future of elections and politics in the United States, and outline ideas for additional research. We believe that our analysis of nationalized politics in both state and congressional elections will help us understand the underlying causes and effects of this important change in American politics. Although down-ticket candidates have always been beholden to those individuals at the top of the ticket, this takes on a very different meaning in an era when ideologically extreme and populist candidates are seeking the highest offices in the land.

# 2

# Nationalized Elections

*A Review*

If 20th-century electoral politics could be summarized with a single phrase, the political adage "All politics is local," which is commonly attributed to former Speaker of the House Tip O'Neill, would be a fitting choice. The often quoted phrase can be understood to mean that "a politician's success is directly tied to his ability to understand and influence the issues of his constituents. . . . [P]ersonal issues, rather than big and intangible ideas, are often what voters care most about."[1] Whether one looks to the regional and corresponding ideological divisions within both major political parties (Aldrich 2010) or the cultivation of the personal vote among one's constituents (Cain, Ferejohn, and Fiorina 1987; Mayhew 1974b), there is ample evidence that local circumstances were crucial to understanding election outcomes in the previous century. During the first few decades of the 21st century, however, American electoral politics have transformed considerably, and the value of local attentiveness has waned (Kaslovsky 2022). As a result, the idea that all politics are in fact local "has been put to the test" as constituents and activists are "drowning out local issues and forcing senators and representatives to answer locally for every national controversy."[2]

The nationalization of politics is not confined to federal elections. In August 2020, the candidates for the nonpartisan mayoral race in Montevallo, Alabama, a town of 6,674 people, were asked to discuss how they would work with local law enforcement if elected. One candidate, Joyce Jones, answered that "she would consider adding social programs to help the town not just respond to crime . . . but prevent it, too."[3] By the next morning, Jones was accused of wanting to "defund the police," a slogan that came to prominence in the summer of 2020 during nationwide protests as part of the Black Lives Matter movement. While Jones attempted to dispel the rumors, the incident was only one in a series of partisan and nationally tinged episodes that defined the campaign. Early in her campaign, Jones was on a door-to-door canvass when she was asked who she was going to vote for in the upcoming presidential election. Another citizen explicitly asked Jones not to support the president in the November election. In lieu of traditional local issues like parks, libraries, roads, and sewers, this election was ultimately defined by national debates on policing and identity politics.

In recent years, political scientists have amassed a vast array of empirical evidence to corroborate the shift away from localized to nationalized elections that is illustrated by the Montevallo mayoral race, among many others. In this chapter, we provide an overview of the extant research on the role of national forces in American electoral politics. We focus on the two primary means through which politics are nationalized: the nature and scope of issue conflict and electoral politics.[4] While the latter is of more immediate interest for our project, it is important to review and understand both dimensions of nationalization (Hopkins 2018). We begin by outlining prior research on how national issues intrude into partisan conflict and electoral politics before reviewing research on the nationalization of electoral outcomes and vote choice.

## NATIONALIZED ISSUE CONFLICT

The scope of political conflict not only plays a central role in the construction of political coalitions (Schattschneider 1960), but it can also determine the nature of electoral competition and political engagement. When national issues are dominant, as during the past few decades, electoral politics through all, or at least most, levels will hinge on national issues such as presidential politics or national political parties. If local issues are more salient to the public, however, then electoral politics should be more likely to be contested in terms of more parochial forces like candidate-specific attributes, such as incumbency or candidate ideology, or locally defined policies. Relatedly, local or regional issues can be viewed through the lens of national politics, which makes discussions of such issues more similar in scope across the nation.

Prior research has identified two pathways through which issue conflict can be more or less national in focus. First, voter knowledge about and engagement with politics can be more nationally focused. Hopkins (2018) argues that politics becomes more nationalized when voters are more knowledgeable about or focused on national politics rather than local politics. Under this arrangement, "national and local politics are fought over related dimensions" and "citizens allocate disproportionate time and attention to the national level" (34–35). As a result of this greater national focus, the scope of conflict among citizens is much wider, while political engagement among voters is more likely to be national in orientation.

Drutman (2018) raises a similar point and notes that "99 percent of respondents in a typical media market never visited websites dedicated to local news." Voters simply do not place much, if any, weight on local issues. As a result, "elections these days, at every level of government, increasingly operate as a singular referendum on the president" (Drutman 2018). However, Trussler's (2021) evaluation of the phased-in distribution of broadband internet service finds that as the information environment evolved and citizens were able to consume news from additional sources besides local news outlets, voters began to prioritize national over subnational issues. Therefore, the evolution of the news environment offers another potential explanation for voters' increased attention to the national at the expense of the local (Martin and McCrain 2019; Moskowitz 2021).

Second, the public's evaluation of politics can depend more on national considerations than on local context. One of the most prominent national factors is the president, and there is considerable evidence that a host of political judgments are impacted by evaluations of the occupant of the White House (Amira 2022; Hopkins and Noel 2022; Sievert and Hinojosa 2022). Jacobson (2019b) finds that the president serves as an important reference point in the public's perceptions of the political parties, and this connection has only strengthened over time. The influence of presidential politics on electoral politics can even extend beyond national elections.

While there is mixed evidence about the strength of the connection between presidential approval and gubernatorial evaluations in the 1980s and 1990s (Atkeson and Partin 1995; Carsey and Wright 1998; Simon 1989), the connection has strengthened in recent years (Brown 2010; Hopkins 2018; Sievert and McKee 2019). Similarly, retrospective voting in federal, state, and local offices depends on "whether or not [candidates] share a partisan label with the president" (Benedictis-Kessner and Warshaw 2020, 627). In this way, the nationalization of issue conflict makes it increasingly difficult for elected officials from the president's party to separate themselves from the nation's chief executive in the mind of the public for better or worse.

A related phenomenon is the intrusion of national issues or identities into otherwise localized politics. For example, national politics and outside donors have become increasingly central to both congressional contents (Sievert and Mathiasen 2023) and local school board elections (Reckhow et al. 2017). As a result of these nationally oriented forces, "school board campaigns that attract outside donors are shaped by trends affecting national political campaigns" rather than the local issues facing the given school district (Reckhow et al. 2017, 803). Similarly, Hopkins (2018, 89) finds that our increasingly nationalized polity is "not one in which place is irrelevant... but nationalization does mean that the salient, divisive issues in politics are likely to be the same across otherwise disparate places." As a result, ostensibly local issues turn out to divide people along familiar national lines regardless of where they live.

In short, the relative weight given to and the relevance of national and local issues are central to understanding how Americans evaluate politics. As voters become increasingly partisan or nationally oriented in their understanding of politics, they will tend to reward candidates who are politically oriented similarly to themselves and punish those who are not. In this vein, Jacobson (2015b, 2015c, 2017) suggests that elections are now regularly referenda on the state of the economy and the president's job performance, as evidenced in many national elections beginning in the late 1990s. Regardless of which of the mechanisms outlined above is the driving force behind more nationalized political behavior, the behavior of the American electorate has resulted in increasingly nationalized outcomes.

## NATIONALIZED ELECTORAL POLITICS

In the realm of electoral politics, nationalization implies an increased correspondence between national-level politics (e.g., presidential elections) and subpresidential elections. While political scientists have used a variety of measures to evaluate nationalization (see, e.g., Claggett, Flanigan, and Zingale 1984; Claggett 1987; Jacobson 2015c; Kawato 1987; Vertz, Frendreis, and Gibson 1987),[5] our primary focus is on the nationalization of vote choice and election outcomes. As Hopkins (2018) notes, there are many ways that subnational elections can become more nationalized. With respect to vote choice and election outcomes, however, nationalization is typically thought of as a process in which top-down forces exert greater influence on the choices voters make at the polls and subsequent election outcomes as compared to candidate-specific characteristics or local forces. In other words, voters have come to rely less on localized factors such as candidate attributes (i.e., background or elective experience) when choosing who to vote for on election day, and more on factors such as which party currently resides in the White House. This tends to result in a greater likelihood of "wave" elections, especially during the midterm, if voters are largely unsatisfied with the party in power but can only take out their frustrations on those candidates on the ballot. In short, in subnational elections, factors like incumbency or candidate ideology become subordinate to factors like an individual's partisanship or preferred choice for president during periods of greater nationalization.

## Vote Choice

The relationship between partisan identification and vote choice has been well documented in the study of American politics (Bartels 2000; Campbell et al. 1960; Key 1966; Hetherington 2001; Smidt 2017). While many voters will support the same party across all electoral contests, there will be some who choose to support a candidate from a different party in at least one race. Scholars have used the incidence of split-ticket voting to better understand the relative weight of national-level forces, such as presidential vote choice or partisanship, and race-specific context, like candidate ideology or incumbency (Born 2008; Burden and Kimball 2004; Davis and Mason 2016; Engstrom and Kernell 2005, 2014; Jacobson 2015c; Sievert and McKee 2019). According to Burden and Kimball (2004, 13), "most straight-ticket voters are loyal partisans who have generally made their voting decisions long before Election Day, even before the official campaign has started." By contrast, the propensity of voters to support candidates from a different party in down-ballot races is a crucial factor in both the existence and the magnitude of the incumbency advantage (Born 2008; Jacobson 2015c).

It follows, then, that the rates of straight-ticket or split-ticket voting will change as elections become more nationalized. These patterns are most likely to be driven by increased partisan sorting (Davis and Mason 2016; Levendusky 2009; Sievert and Banda 2022), negative attitudes toward the opposing party (Abramowitz and Webster 2016; Bankert 2020), and higher levels of polarization among the most politically engaged (Abramowitz 2010; Hare and Poole 2014). As a result, many voters decide they will vote a straight ticket early in the election season, and those who are less likely to display this behavior are some of the least engaged and therefore least likely to cast a ballot. The result is national politics dictating the outcomes of subnational elections (Abramowitz and Webster 2016; Jacobson 2015c, 2019b; Hopkins 2018; Sievert and McKee 2019). That is precisely what Fiorina (2016, 1) observes: "[S]plit-ticket voting and the incumbency advantage have declined and party candidates in different arenas increasingly tend to win and lose together." Why would voters engage in such behavior? One explanation offered by Fiorina (2016) is that voters no longer have liberal Republicans or conservative Democrats to vote for. Therefore, voting behavior is likely to look more nationalized and partisan based on the options presented to voters (on this point, see also Thomsen 2014).

## Election Outcomes

Whether measured in terms of the partisan outcome of an election or the correlation between partisan vote shares across competitions, there is also ample evidence of nationalization in aggregate election outcomes across a variety of subpresidential contests (Abramowitz and Webster 2016; Amlani and Algara 2021; Carson, Sievert, and Williamson 2020; Hopkins 2018; Jacobson 2015c; Jacobson and Carson 2020; Sievert and McKee 2019). The connection between national forces and election outcomes is perhaps most readily apparent in congressional elections. As the electoral advantages of incumbency declined in recent House and Senate elections, there has been a corresponding increase in the impact of the presidential contest on congressional elections (Abramowitz and Webster 2016; Jacobson 2015c; Sievert and McKee 2019). One notable consequence of this development is the near disappearance of legislators who serve in districts or states that were carried by the other party's presidential candidate (Jacobson and Carson 2020).

Even special elections, which necessarily take place without the president at the top of the ballot, are subject to national political considerations (Knotts and Ragusa 2016). These trends are particularly noteworthy because these contests were once far more isolated from national forces. Knotts and Ragusa (2016, 22) find that "presidential approval is predictive of special election outcomes" and that "the effect of presidential approval on special election outcomes has increased in magnitude from 1995 to 2014." Bullock and Owen (2021) take this point even further by noting that special elections often occur because of the unexpected death or resignation of a representative, thrusting national attention upon the election because it is the only one occurring at that time and place.[6]

There is also evidence that presidential politics have begun to structure the outcome in many state-level races. Both Hopkins (2018) and Sievert and McKee (2019) find evidence of an increased correspondence between presidential and gubernatorial election outcomes, which reinforces earlier evidence of the connection between evaluations of the president and vote choice in gubernatorial contests (Carsey and Wright 1998; Simon 1989). Despite more nationalized gubernatorial contests, Sievert and McKee (2019) do find that these elections are still more insulated from national forces than are congressional elections. Governors are not the only state-level election officials, however, whose electoral fortunes are now closely tied to presidential politics. Several studies have found a connection between presidential and state legislative elections (Abramowitz and Webster 2016; Jacobson 2019b; Melusky and Richman 2020; Rogers 2016; Zingher and Richman 2019). Zingher and Richman (2019, 1036) contend that "state legislative election outcomes are determined by states' orientations toward the national parties." This trend appears to be increasing as well, as Melusky and Richman (2020, 441) argue that "nationalization reached a new peak in its influence on state legislative elections in 2018." In addition to state legislative elections, Weinschenk et al. (2020, 1) find that "presidential vote share influences voting in state supreme court contests," and this effect is even present in nonpartisan elections.

For additional context, consider the 2022 election cycle. Though Trump was no longer president, his presence loomed large over many races. Senate races in Alabama and Ohio featured Republican candidates jockeying for the title of the most "Trumpian" candidate. In the Alabama Republican primary, Representative Mo Brooks, who initially won the endorsement of Trump, faced off against numerous candidates for U.S. senator, most notably Katie Britt and Mike Durant. Britt had served as retiring incumbent senator Richard Shelby's chief of staff as well as the president and CEO of the Business Council of Alabama. Durant was an army veteran whose service in the military inspired the film *Black Hawk Down*. Before the primary election, Brooks's campaign was gradually losing its lead on the field, and Trump ultimately rescinded his endorsement, claiming he did so because Brooks did not more ardently support Trump's false claims of election fraud in the 2020 presidential election.[7] After the first round of voting, Britt led both Brooks and Durant but did not secure enough of the vote to win outright. This led to a runoff between Britt and Brooks, in which Britt was the clear favorite. Shortly before the runoff, Trump offered his endorsement to Britt, and she would go on to win handily.[8] In this case, Trump's endorsement, un-endorsement, and re-endorsement were all tied to which candidate was most likely to prevail at the time, a phenomenon we will explore in more depth in Chapter 8. Nonetheless, the campaign still centered around issues related to Trump and national politics instead of more state-specific or candidate-centric factors as we might expect, all else being equal.

In Ohio, Trump's effect on the outcome of the 2022 primaries may have been even more pronounced. The race for U.S. senator featured many candidates, Josh Mandel and J. D. Vance being the most prominent. The two actively sought Trump's endorsement, as it could prove decisive in such a fractured field. Despite lacking support from the Republican establishment, Vance won the support of Trump, his son Donald Trump Jr., and wealthy donor Peter Theil.[9] In a race with seven candidates, including four vying to be seen as the best Trump acolyte, that support proved to be enough for Vance to win 32 percent of the vote as well as the nomination. As reported by BBC News, "Republicans across the US continue to demonstrate respect for, or fear of, Mr. Trump's political influence."[10] Though it is unclear whether the Trump endorsement was determinative of the outcome, it is clear that national politics and figures like Trump were an unavoidable issue for Republicans seeking the Senate nomination in Ohio and elsewhere around the county.

As previously mentioned, nationalization is not limited to federal offices. Given Trump's oft repeated but unfounded claims that the 2020 election were fraudulent, several candidates for secretary of state based their campaigns around his allegations and employed similar rhetoric.[11] As the chief election officer with oversight of elections in 40 of the 50 states, this position was ripe for candidates to focus on issues related to election security and integrity and perpetuate Trump's narrative in the process. As one analyst notes, the secretary of state has not traditionally been "a very high-profile office." Given the rise in nationalization coupled with Trump's election fraud claims, these positions have taken on an even greater level of importance.[12] These candidates are not, however, focusing on improving state-specific election processes (such as allowing preprocessing of mail-in ballots in Pennsylvania, which led to a delay in the vote count there in 2020). Instead, they have devoted their time and attention to issues related to national conversations around elections, such as false claims of massive illegal votes that were adjudicated in postelection audits. These candidates are one of the enduring legacies of Trump's claims about election irregularity in 2020 that will likely continue so long as electoral politics remain nationalized.

## SUMMARY

Given the pervasiveness of nationalization and the substantial research that currently exists on the topic, it is important to discuss the impact of nationalization on American politics. Though it may seem counterintuitive, this is arguably a logical step taken by parties to facilitate mobilization and vote choice by citizens. As Rogowski and Tucker (2018, 83) show, "ideological predictability substantially increases electoral support." Therefore, fielding candidates who are consistent in their rhetoric and priorities across different levels of government increases parties' overall chances of success. This also allows voters to make a (relatively) well-informed decision with a minimal amount of information. However, this strategy is not without other, potentially negative consequences. If national conditions override candidate characteristics, we should necessarily see a decrease in the incumbency advantage, for instance. Additionally, as Hopkins (2018) notes, nationalization and polarization may be closely related, among both political elites as well as the electorate. Given the preceding discussion, we therefore investigate these dynamics further for all elections between 1840 and 2020 in the following chapters.

Additionally, we argue that it is important to put this recent nationalization into a broader historical context. Most of the research on this topic has focused on the recent increase in the nationalization of elections, and for good reason, since it has been a long time since elections in the United States were strongly influenced by who was at the top of the ticket. However, as previously mentioned, this is not the first time in American political history that nationalization has been so prevalent. The institutions that were in place during the 19th century (like the party ballot) necessarily induced high levels of partisan loyalty among those voting, especially since voting was not done in private, as is the case today. Voters had a difficult time splitting their tickets in those instances where they might want to vote for one party for president and a different party for subnational offices since the ballots and electoral rules in place largely discouraged such behavior (Engstrom and Kernell 2014; Ware 2002).

To further illustrate the effects of nationalization on elections over an extended period of time, we evaluate congressional races between 1840 and 2020—the first study of this kind, to our knowledge. These historical elections serve as a counterfactual of sorts, which provides us with additional analytical leverage when investigating the effect of nationalization on various electoral phenomena. More specifically, they give us the opportunity to explore nationalization caused by distinct factors in different political eras to better understand how nationalization might lead to similar outcomes even though the underlying causes may be unique. In the next chapter, we focus on various ways to measure nationalization before shifting our attention to more systematic, empirical analyses in the remainder of the book.

# 3
# Evidence of Nationalization across Time

In 1872, Republican president Ulysses S. Grant ran for a second term and easily defeated his Democratic opponent, Horace Greeley, who died following the election and prior to the Electoral College votes being cast. Along with Grant's significant electoral victory, the Republicans managed to pick up 61 seats in the U.S. House of Representatives, which provided them with a sizable advantage over the Democrats in the 43rd Congress. Two years later, however, the Republicans' electoral fortunes quickly changed. The 1874 midterm elections were held during a deep economic depression that had begun in 1873, along with growing allegations of corruption within the Grant administration.[1] After all the votes were tallied, Republicans ended up losing 92 seats in the House along with majority control of the chamber because of the highly nationalized election. This was the second largest swing in the control of seats in the House (the largest occurring in 1894) but represented the greatest loss of seats ever for the Republican Party (Dubin 1998).

Fast-forward 134 years. Barack Obama, the first African American president in history, is selected by a majority of voters in the historic 2008 election on the platform "Hope and Change." The Democrats had previously made gains in Congress in the 2006 midterms and added to their totals in 2008. Two years later, the Democrats' congressional gains from the two previous elections were erased in the 2010 midterms. In that

*Nationalized Politics*. Jamie L. Carson, Joel Sievert, and Ryan D. Williamson, Oxford University Press.
© Oxford University Press 2024. DOI: 10.1093/oso/9780197669655.003.0003

election, Republicans picked up 63 seats in the U.S. House, which was their best showing in over 60 years and gave them a 242–193 seat majority. Democratic candidates in 2010 were linked to President Obama and were evaluated negatively based on both the economy and the president's job performance. Republicans were effective at framing the election as a referendum on the president, especially with respect to the controversial Affordable Care Act (frequently referred to as Obamacare), which was something Obama had campaigned on in 2008. Thus, what was clearly a legislative victory ended up being viewed as a political failure by Republicans and a majority of voters who went to the polls in 2010 (Jacobson and Carson 2020).

Although separated by well over a century, both midterm elections reflect a highly nationalized political context that resulted in significant electoral defeats for members of the president's party. In 1874, Democrats were able to nationalize the election by taking advantage of the economic recession and the growing unpopularity of President Grant because of the increasing perception of corruption in his administration. During the 2010 midterms, Republicans portrayed Obamacare as "socialized" medicine that would lead to government takeover of the healthcare industry and voters bought into this message. The fact that both elections were highly nationalized despite their very different political eras highlights the significance of nationalization in influencing congressional elections, which is the focus of this chapter.

## CONGRESSIONAL ELECTIONS IN HISTORICAL CONTEXT

Since one of the primary contributions of this book is to analyze a longer historical time span than in previous studies, it is necessary to provide a brief background on electoral politics in earlier historical periods. Elections from the 1840s through the early 20th century are of particular importance because they are starkly different from modern elections (Bensel 2004). One prominent example is that of Abraham Lincoln. Indeed, unlike many other politicians from his era, Lincoln was considered incredibly ambitious when it came to obtaining political office. At the age of 23, he first sought election to the Illinois General Assembly but lost in August 1832 (most likely a function of his youth and inexperience). Two years later he ran again, but this time was successfully elected to his first term in the Illinois House of Representatives. He was reelected to the seat in 1836 and 1838 but was defeated in December 1838 in his bid to become Speaker of the Illinois House. Nevertheless, Lincoln continued to demonstrate political ambition, as reflected by his service as Whig floor leader during the next two years. He sought a fourth term to the Illinois House in 1840 and was subsequently reelected but declined to be a candidate for renomination two years later, in 1842.

In May 1846, Lincoln sought the Whig Party nomination for the Seventh Congressional District in Illinois and was elected in August of that year. He ended up serving only one term in the U.S. House and chose not to seek renomination in 1848, most likely due to the principle of rotation in office that was the norm for the Whig Party at the time. Had he been given the opportunity to seek renomination by his party, he likely would have won and most likely would have continued winning given his ambition and prior political experience. In November 1854, Lincoln was again elected to the Illinois House but declined to serve and decided to seek a seat in the U.S. Senate instead. Despite his experience serving in the Illinois legislature, he lost his bid for the Senate in February 1855, when the legislature elected Lyman Trumbull instead. Lincoln was chosen four years later as a candidate for the Senate by the newly formed Republican Party, but ultimately lost the election to Stephen Douglas. He did not have the opportunity to run again for the Illinois General Assembly or the U.S. Congress since he was nominated by the Republican Party as their candidate for president in 1860—which he ultimately won.

Prior to the adoption of the Australian ballot in the late 19th century and direct primary in the early 20th century, parties themselves were responsible for selecting candidates as well as printing and distributing ballots (Engstrom and Kernell 2005, 2014; Rusk 1970; Ware 2002). These party-supplied ballots are of note for two reasons. First, the party ticket listed every candidate on the party's electoral slate (Rusk 1970; Ware 2002), which meant that voters were left on election day to choose between *parties* rather than between *candidates*. Although it was technically possible to cast a split ticket during this period, the parties went to great lengths to prevent such behavior (Bensel 2004; Rusk 1970; Ware 2002). Second, since the parties controlled who appeared on the ballot, office seekers needed party support to be elected, which meant political careers took on a different form during this period. Rather than progressing through a clear office hierarchy, as we typically observe in the modern era, ambitious politicians had political careers that spanned many types of offices across different levels of government (Carson and Sievert 2018; MacKenzie 2015), as evidenced by Lincoln's career.

The institutional and partisan structure of early American elections led scholars to conclude that these earlier periods were not comparable to contemporary elections. While this perspective was dominant in congressional and electoral studies for many years, several studies from the past two decades have challenged the prior scholarly consensus. First, the conventional wisdom held that there should be little role for individual candidates throughout much of the 19th century. The electoral institutions of this era—the party ballot and party nomination convention in particular—created a more party-oriented electoral process (Engstrom and Kernell 2005, 2014; Rusk 1970). As such, the party's control over nominations and central role in election administration are often assumed to have left little room for candidates to matter. Some scholars have therefore argued that an electoral role for individual candidates was limited until reforms like the Australian ballot and the direct primary fostered an environment in which higher levels of candidate-specific effects could be observed (Carson and Williamson 2018a). In addition to electoral institutions that limited the role of individual candidates, many 19th-century legislators are thought to have had little interest in a career in Congress (Polsby 1968), which meant they had few incentives to develop a personal vote like their more modern counterparts. Second, some scholars contend that voters during this period were not concerned with factors like candidate experience or legislative actions. Instead, 19th-century voters are portrayed as voting almost exclusively based on party affiliation (Skeen 1986) and as generally not holding public officials accountable for their behavior in office (Formisano 1974; Swift 1987).

A growing body of research, however, suggests individual candidates played an important role in structuring the outcome of 19th-century elections. While congressional careers were shorter throughout the century (Polsby 1968; Kernell 1977b), Carson and Sievert (2018, 84) find that most incumbents ran for reelection during this period, which means the "modal election pitted an incumbent against a challenger." Even though the incumbent win rate was lower in earlier historical periods than it is today, incumbents have outperformed nonincumbents since at least the 1820s (Carson and Sievert 2018). Similarly, prior electoral experience could boost a candidate's electoral fortune throughout the party ballot era (Carson and Hood 2014; Carson and Roberts 2013; Carson and Sievert 2017).

Although Progressive Era electoral reforms did enhance the value of candidate-specific attributes (Carson and Roberts 2013), these reforms were not a necessary condition for the individual candidates to impact election outcomes. Since the party ballot was a collective good that benefited a party's entire slate of candidates (Carson and Roberts 2013), parties had an incentive to recruit the strongest possible ticket. The likelihood of defeating an incumbent during this period was always higher when a party managed to recruit a higher quality candidate than when they failed to do so (Carson and Roberts 2013; Carson and Sievert 2018). Recruiting better, more experienced candidates could even produce spillover effects in other races, which included reverse coattails in presidential contests (Carson and Sievert 2017). The addition of a strong congressional candidate could also boost voter turnout, which could, in turn, increase electoral competition in incumbent-contested races (Carson and Sievert 2018).

Elections held during the 20th century and beyond are now largely candidate-centered contests at an institutional level because parties do not control nominations or election administration the way they once did, and voters choose between candidates rather than parties for individual office. Nevertheless, vote choice and election outcomes in recent decades have become increasingly party-centered despite the more permissive institutional arrangements (Hopkins 2018). Based on the decline of split-ticket voting and a resurgence in mass partisanship, congressional elections are far more nationalized than in previous decades (Davis and Mason 2016; Hopkins 2018; Jacobson 2015c; Sievert and McKee 2019). In this regard, elections have become as much about which candidate is at the top of the ticket as was the case throughout the latter part of the 19th century.

## NATIONALIZATION OVER TIME

Despite the many differences between historical and modern elections, they share a common dynamic in the form of nationalized electoral politics. Elections held during the 19th century, for instance, were nationalized because of the party ballot in use that forced voters to primarily vote a straight ticket when they went to the polls. Today, by contrast, voters are less likely to split their tickets not because of specific institutional arrangements but due to shifts in voter behavior or strengthened partisanship (Abramowitz and Webster 2016; Davis and Mason 2016; Jacobson 2015c). To help demonstrate both the similarities and differences across these two historical periods and general patterns in nationalization, we review some of the recent literature that examines trends across the two political eras.

### Presidential and Congressional Election Outcomes

We begin by examining the relationship between presidential and congressional election outcomes, which is a commonly employed measure of nationalization (Abramowitz and Webster 2016; Jacobson 2015c; Sievert and McKee 2019) across the entire time of our study. The top panel of Figure 3.1 reports the correlation between the district-level Democratic share of the vote for presidential and congressional elections from 1840 to 2020. We report the correlations separately for presidential (solid black

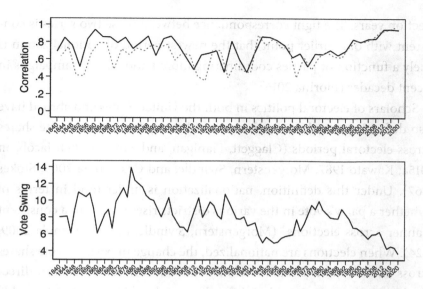

**Figure 3.1** Correlation between Presidential and Congressional Vote Share and Interelection Democratic Vote Swing
NOTE: The solid black line in the top panel denotes presidential election years; the dashed gray line represents midterm election years.

line) and midterm (dashed gray line) election years. There are several notable patterns in the top panel of Figure 3.1. First, the correlation between presidential and congressional elections is quite high throughout the party-ballot era and, at times, reaches levels comparable to the modern era.[2] There is a marked drop in correlation though during midterm election years, which comports with the idea of an institutions-induced nationalization.

Second, while the two series begin to track each other more closely in the post-party-ballot period, there are still several instances in which the correlation rises during presidential years before dropping during midterm elections. Similarly, the overall correlation between the two drops during the early 20th century. The growing disconnect between presidential and congressional elections is consistent with the rise of localized factors noted in other studies (Jacobson 2015c). Third, since 1968 the correlation between presidential and congressional vote not only has increased, but there have been few differences between presidential and midterm election years. The tight correspondence between these two series is consistent with our earlier point that the newest period of nationalization is likely a function of parties coordinating more nationalized campaigns in recent decades (Fiorina 2016).

Scholars of electoral politics in both the United States and abroad have also defined nationalization in terms of "swings" in partisan vote shares across electoral periods (Claggett, Flanigan, and Zingale 1984; Jacobson 2015a; Kawato 1987; Morgenstern, Swindle, and Castagnola 2009; Stokes 1967). Under this definition, nationalization is understood in terms of "whether a party's vote in the various districts rises or falls in a consistent manner across elections" (Morgenstern, Swindle, and Castagnola 2009, 1324). When elections are nationalized, the change in partisan vote shares across two elections should not only move in the same partisan direction between two contests, but these changes should be also be of roughly similar magnitude. For example, a five-point shift in district-level vote in the Republican direction in every electoral unit between two elections would be evidence of perfect nationalization. As elections become less nationalized, we should observe differences in the direction or magnitude (or both) of partisan vote swing.

We follow standard practice and measure the interelection vote swing as the difference in district-level partisan vote shares across consecutive elections. For our analysis, we began by calculating the district-level Democratic vote swing as the difference between the party's vote share in consecutive elections. Since redistricting prevents us from examining stable districts, we exclude instances in which congressional district lines were redrawn. Most notably, this means we are forced to exclude the first election following the decennial reapportionment of congressional districts. Although prior studies have examined both the mean and the variance of the partisan swing (Kawato 1987; Stokes 1967), the latter quantity is of more immediate interest for studies of nationalization since it quantifies the uniformity of swing across the various electoral districts. We therefore calculated the standard deviation of the Democratic vote swing for each election year. As the forgoing discussion indicates, a high standard deviation is, according to prior studies, evidence of less nationalized elections, while a lower standard deviation is consistent with more nationalized elections.

The bottom panel of Figure 3.1 reports the standard deviation of the Democratic vote swing between 1840 and 2020. The data for the post–World War II period mirrors prior studies that found the interelection vote swing began to increase in the 1940s (Stokes 1967) from a standard deviation around 4 to 5 points to a standard deviation of around 8 to 10 points in the 1980s (Jacobson 2015a) and peaked in the 1980s before reaching historical lows in the past few elections (Jacobson 2015a). From its modern peak, the interelection swing has fallen nearly monotonically over the past several decades and is now at historic lows, with a standard deviation around 4 points.

Once we move beyond modern elections, however, interelection swing provides a somewhat different account of patterns of nationalization than those observed in the top panel of Figure 3.1. First, elections at the turn of the 20th century appeared to be marginally less nationalized, like those in the 1950s and 1990s. The standard deviation of the Democratic swing was several points lower in the first decade of the century though with a low of 6.3 points in 1908. As we move forward in time, though, the standard deviation of the Democratic swing rises back up to around 8 to 10 points from the 1910s through the 1930s. These patterns contrast with spikes in the correlation between presidential and congressional voting in the 1920s and 1930s.

Second, the interelection swing was, on average, higher throughout the 19th century. There are two periods—1850 to 1856 and 1874 to 1890—when the standard deviation of the Democratic swing is more than 10 points. While it drops to around 6 points in three presidential election years, the measure is above 8 points in the remaining elections. Based on the measure of interelection swing, we would conclude that every single election in the 19th century was *less nationalized* than nearly every election since the New Deal. As the top panel in Figure 3.1 makes clear, however, the correlation between presidential and congressional voting was higher in most modern elections until the past two decades. Indeed, the correlation coefficient between presidential and congressional vote share was approximately 0.80 in 10 of the 15 presidential elections between 1840 and 1896. It was not until the 1996 election, though, that the correlation between presidential and congressional voting was consistently more than 0.80.[3]

To further explore these discrepancies, it can be helpful to examine the Democratic swing in elections from these different historical eras. For now, we focus on a comparison of the 1856 and 2008 elections. These years provide an interesting basis for comparison because the correlations between district-level presidential and congressional vote shares are nearly identical in both years: 0.83 for 1856 and 0.84 for 2008. Based on these correlation coefficients, we would conclude that these two years were equally nationalized. The standard deviation of the Democratic swing is nearly 5 points higher, though, in 1856 than in 2008, 10.9 and 6.0, respectively. If we relied exclusively on the measure of interelection swing, we would conclude that 1856 was far less nationalized than 2008. More important, we would also have to infer that the 1856 election was less nationalized than *every* election in the 20th and 21st century.

Figure 3.2 plots the distribution of the Democratic swing for the 1856 and 2008 presidential elections. For both years, the mean swing is above zero, which is not surprising since the Democratic Party won a majority of the House seats and control of the White House in both years. What is of more immediate interest is the shape of the distribution of the Democratic swing in each year. In 1856, the distribution is much more dispersed than it was in 2008. The minimum swing was −29 in 1856 compared to −21.7 in 2008, while the maximum swing was 40.5 in 1856 and 22.2 in 2008. Indeed, 11 percent of the observations in 1856 are similar to or larger in magnitude than the minimum and maximum values for the 2008 Democratic swing.

In sum, these two conventional measures of nationalization provide notably different conclusions about the nationalization of congressional elections across time. Based on the correlation between presidential and congressional vote shares, we would conclude that many elections throughout the 19th century, particularly those that coincided with a presidential contest, and the early 21st century were highly nationalized. If we rely instead on the interelection swing, however, we infer that although

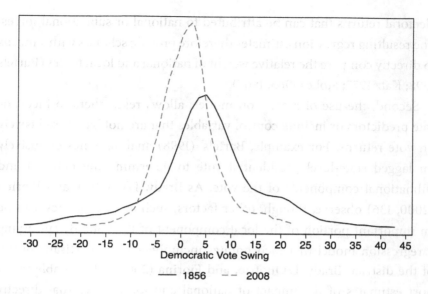

Figure 3.2 Comparison of Democratic Vote Swing in Different Electoral Eras

congressional elections have witnessed an ebb and flow in the level of nationalization, the past two decades are effectively historical outliers. The latter conclusion is potentially problematic for our current project since our objective is to examine nationalized politics across time. We therefore believe it is prudent to review one last measure of nationalization, which helps shed light on the differences observed in our first two measures of nationalization.

## Local and National Forces

Both previous measures of nationalization are descriptive and do not provide a means to control for or assess the relative impact of national and local forces. Several studies have turned to regression models to address this shortcoming of the more descriptive measures (Bartels 1998; Brady, D'Onofrio, and Fiorina 2000; Katz 1973; Stokes 1965, 1967). There are two key advantages of a regression-based measurement of nationalization. First, regression models allow a researcher to parcel out the variance in electoral returns that can be attributed to national or subnational forces. The resulting regression estimates therefore provide scholars with a means to directly compare the relative weight of national and local forces (Bartels 1998; Katz 1973; Stokes 1965, 1967).

Second, the use of regression models allows researchers to incorporate predictors or include control variables that are not based exclusively on vote returns. For example, Bartels' (1998) analysis relies exclusively on lagged state-level presidential vote to determine the national and subnational components of the vote. As Brady, D'Onofrio, and Fiorina (2000, 136) observe, though, other factors, such as incumbency, can be an important portion of the local component of the vote. By specifying a regression model that incorporates incumbency and partisan control of the district, Brady, D'Onofrio, and Fiorina (2000, 141) are able to report estimates of the impact of national and local forces that directly control for district and candidate-specific effects that might be separate from the conventional measures used to capture national and subnational dynamics.

For the analysis in this section, we replicate the Brady, D'Onofrio, and Fiorina (2000) model for each election year in the period under study. Brady, D'Onofrio, and Fiorina's regression model is a modified version of Gelman and King's (1990) incumbency advantage estimator, and we outline the parameters of this model in Equation 3.1.[4] The outcome variable for this linear regression model is the Democratic share of the two-party vote in district $i$ during election $t$. Local forces are captured by inclusion of the lagged Democratic vote share. Since the use of lagged vote requires stable districts, we are forced to exclude elections or districts immediately following redistricting. National forces are incorporated into the model through the district-level presidential vote. The relative weight of national and local forces can therefore be assessed by examining the coefficient estimates for $\beta_1$ (local) and $\beta_2$ (national). In addition to these measures, the model also includes covariates to account for partisan control of the district (+1 for a Democratic district and −1 for a Republican district) and the incumbency status (+1 for a Democratic incumbent, 0 for open seat, and −1 for a Republican incumbent).

$$\text{Dem. Vote}_{it} = \beta_0 + \beta_1 \text{ Dem. Vote}_{it-1} + \beta_2 \text{ Dem. Pres. Vote}_{it}$$
$$+ \beta_3 \text{ Party}_{it} + \beta_4 \text{ Inc.}_{it} + \epsilon_{it} \quad (3.1)$$

We estimate this model for each election year from 1840 to 2020, following Brady, D'Onofrio, and Fiorina's approach, and we report the estimates separately for presidential and midterm election years. In Figure 3.3, we report the coefficient estimates for local forces in the top two panels and national forces in the bottom two, along with their corresponding 95 percent confidence intervals. We also separate presidential elections (the two left panels) and midterm elections (the two right panels). There are several notable patterns evident in these findings. First, during the mid- to late 19th century, when the party ballot was in use, the estimates for national forces were at their peak. Between 1840 and 1888, the coefficient estimate for the national component was greater than 0.75 in 6 of 10 elections and was approximately 0.7 in three additional elections. Substantively, this means that an increase of 10 points in the Democratic

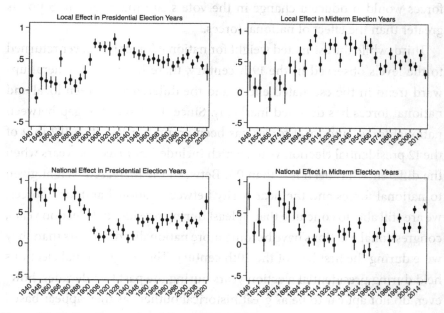

Figure 3.3 National versus Local Forces, 1840–2020

presidential vote yielded a 7- to 8-point change in the congressional vote. Furthermore, the estimated weight of local forces compared to national forces was lower in each election year in the 19th century except for the 1868 election. It is also of note that the estimate for local forces is negative in 1844 and is not statistically significant in three of the election years during this period: 1840, 1864, and 1884. Overall, the findings for this period comport with the observation from prior research that the party ballot fostered a near mechanical connection between presidential and subpresidential races (Engstrom and Kernell 2005, 2014).

Second, the relative weight of local and national forces shifts abruptly at the turn of the 20th century. Since the election of 1900, the effect of national forces has been less than the estimate for local forces in each presidential election year. The gap between local and national forces was highest in the first half of the 20th century. In the first 11 presidential years we examined between 1900 and 1948, the difference between the estimate for local and national forces was more than 0.5 points in five election years and was over 0.4 in an additional three. In substantive terms, this means that for an increase of 10 percentage points in the Democratic vote, local forces would produce a change in the vote share that was 4 to 5 points greater than the effect of national forces.

Third, while the estimated weight for national forces has never returned to the levels observed in the 19th century, there has been a general upward trend in the estimated effect, and the difference between local and national forces has declined markedly. Since the 1960s, the gap between national forces and local forces has been around or less than 0.2 in 9 of the 12 presidential election years, which includes four election years when the difference has been less than 0.1. Between the increased weight given to national forces and the near parity between national and local forces, we are still able to conclude that, at least during presidential election years, congressional elections have become more nationalized contests than they were during the first half of the 20th century. The congressional elections held during presidential election years during the past two decades, however, do not appear to be as great historical outliers as they appear based on the first two measures of nationalization.

While the series for presidential election years had a clear pattern across time, the results for midterm years are not as consistent. First, there are several midterm election years—for example, 1846, 1874, and 1878—when the weight of national forces is much larger than the local forces. There are other years, though—such as 1858, 1870, and 1894—when the estimated effect for local forces is greater than those of national forces. In the remaining midterm years in the 19th century, the difference between local and national effects is quite small in magnitude. In short, the relative weight of local context or national trends was not consistent in midterm election years during this period.

Second, the midterm elections of the early and mid-20th century do largely mirror the patterns evident in presidential election years. With a few exceptions (e.g., 1914 and 1954), there is a robust and sizable gap between the local and national estimates, the former clustering between 0.6 and 0.8 from 1906 through the 1960s. The weight of national forces, however, was between 0 and 0.2 in 11 of the 15 elections during this period. The substantive difference between local and national forces was even larger in midterm years during this period than it was in presidential years. For a 10-point change in the Democratic vote, the effect of local forces was between 7 and 8 points higher than the effect of national forces in several contests.

Third, the gap between local and national forces began to close in the 1990s and throughout the start of the 21st century. Although the gap between the local and national forces was as high as 0.6 in 1986 and almost 0.4 as recently as 2006, there are years when national forces have equal or comparable weight to that in midterm years. For example, the estimates of local and national conditions are within a few percentage points of one another in 1994 and effectively identical in 2018, which is perhaps not surprising given scholarly accounts of the dynamics of these elections (Campbell 1997; Jacobson 1996, 2019a). We also observe one midterm year, the 2010 election, when the estimated effect of national forces is *higher* than the weight given to local context. Given the Democrats' infamous "shellacking" that year, the observation that 2010 was an especially nationalized contest is not surprising (Carson and Pettigrew 2013; Jacobson

2011). However, it is interesting to observe that other recent notable midterm years, namely 2006 and 2014, are not as highly nationalized based on this metric as they are for the more descriptive measures discussed earlier.

With respect to the measurement of nationalization, Figure 3.3 leads to two important observations. The first is that modern elections are not nearly as nationalized as contests under the party ballot in use during the 19th century. While congressional elections in presidential years were consistently nationalized throughout that century, the high point of nationalization in midterm elections also appears during this era. These patterns are not surprising when we remember that the electoral institutions in this period led to party-centered elections and made it difficult, but not impossible, for candidates to separate their own electoral fortunes from those of their party. Second, the most recent two decades have witnessed an increased weight for national forces and a declining role for local forces. While the estimate for local forces is still larger than the effect for national forces in most presidential election years, the gap between the two has decreased by a considerable magnitude. The growing importance of national forces along with the waning impact of local factors is consistent with the general expectation of increased nationalization.

## SOURCES OF NATIONALIZED ELECTIONS

Based on our analysis of three different measures of election nationalization, there are two different mechanisms through which electoral politics can become more nationalized. First, the dominance of national forces, such as presidential politics, can be the product of electoral institutions. The party ballot, which was in place during the mid- to late 19th century, ensured that voters were *forced* to choose between parties rather than individual candidates (Engstrom and Kernell 2005, 2014; Rusk 1970). During presidential election years, voter decision-making in many state and local contests was directly tied to national-level politics. When presidential and subpresidential races were held at the same time, the party ballot guaranteed that "coattail voting occurred by default" unless voters went to extraordinary lengths to split their vote (Engstrom and Kernell 2005, 535). While some factors (such as an elongated electoral calendar or midterm elections) weakened the connection between presidential and subpresidential elections (Carson and Sievert 2017, 2018), a candidate's success depended on the strength of his party's presidential candidate when they appeared on the same ballot (Engstrom and Kernell 2005, 2014).

Second, individual-level decisions on Election Day can also lead to more nationalized electoral politics. In the modern era, the president has become an increasingly important reference point for political behavior (Amira 2022; Barber and Pope 2019; Hopkins 2018; Hopkins and Noel 2022; Jacobson 2019a; Sievert and McKee 2019; Sievert and Williamson 2018). One consequence of these developments is that attitudes toward the president are more central to public evaluations of the political parties (Jacobson 2019b), which has the effect of "nationalizing" the party brands (Hopkins 2018). The other implication is that individual-level vote choice across different electoral contests has become more strongly correlated over time (Hopkins 2018; Sievert and McKee 2019). As a result, voters tend to support the same party in presidential and most subpresidential elections (Abramowitz and Webster 2016; Carson, Sievert, and Williamson 2020; Hopkins 2018, Sievert and McKee 2019). The observed increase in party-line voting is driven, at least in part, by partisans becoming increasingly sorted (Davis and Mason 2016; Levendusky 2009). In sum, although the cause of straight-ticket voting differs across time—voter choice rather than institutional design—the electoral consequences are largely the same.

## SUMMARY

As this chapter has illustrated, nationalization can take on distinct forms across different political eras, and the methods that have traditionally been used to measure this concept can yield disparate results depending on the underlying causes of nationalization. Our goal in presenting multiple measures of nationalization has been to demonstrate this so we can better understand both the similarities and the differences in how nationalization is interpreted across time. When higher levels of nationalization are a function of electoral institutions (such as the party ballot), as it was during the 19th century, the consequences may look like those observed in the modern era depending on how it is measured even if the underlying mechanism is different. By contrast, nationalization resulting from individual vote choice may have a more distinct local component, which was clearly not the case during the 19th century when the party ballot was in use. We believe that recognizing and understanding these significant differences across political eras is crucial to identifying the underlying causes and effects of nationalization in the past and the present. In the remainder of the book, we examine several of these causes and effects to elucidate our broader thesis about nationalization.

# 4

# Nationalization and the Electoral Connection

In his foundational book on Congress, Mayhew (1974b, 5) treats legislators as "single-minded seekers of reelection." While acknowledging that this assumption is an overt simplification of reality, he contends that it provides a useful mechanism for explaining many features of the modern Congress. Carson and Jenkins (2011) refined Mayhew's theorizing about the electoral connection and identified four conditions—ambition, autonomy, responsiveness, and accountability—that they suggest are essential to a representative-constituent linkage grounded in elections regardless of the political era under consideration. In this chapter, we focus on the condition of accountability.

Electoral accountability—the use of elections to punish or reward elected officials for their performance in office—is an essential element of representative democracy. While elections are not the only means through which constituents can convey their preferences to or influence members of Congress, they constitute the principal, albeit an imperfect, method of control. The potential for and extent of electoral accountability is therefore an important component of the electoral connection (Carson and Jenkins 2011). When elected officials have no reason to fear retribution on Election Day, there is little reason to expect electoral considerations to inform their decision-making (Arnold 1990).

*Nationalized Politics.* Jamie L. Carson, Joel Sievert, and Ryan D. Williamson, Oxford University Press.
© Oxford University Press 2024. DOI: 10.1093/oso/9780197669655.003.0004

Consider the fact that few political outcomes are more certain than the president's party losing seats in a midterm election. Since 1862, the president's party improved its seat share in only 3 of 40 midterm elections.[1] Throughout much of the 20th century, however, these midterm losses often did little to change the partisan composition of Congress. Only 6 of the 25 midterm elections held in the 20th century witness such change in party control; three—1910, 1918, and 1930—occur in the first three decades, and a 40-year gap exists between the final two instances, in 1954 and 1994. By contrast, the 21st century began with a rare instance of the president's party gaining seats. Since the Democrats regained control of the House in 2006, however, partisan control of the House has changed hands on three more occasions, 2010, 2018, and 2022. What is particularly noteworthy is that two of these three cases—2010 and 2018—were a midterm election in which the president's party suffered significant losses. These changes were not the result of a popular president sweeping his party into power but, instead, were the product of electoral retribution.

Indeed, incumbents from the president's party are not oblivious to the fact that historical trends will likely work against them. For example, former vice president Mike Pence's plan to campaign extensively on behalf of Republican congressional candidates during the 2018 midterm was the result of an early 2018 meeting with congressional Republicans. According to media accounts, House Republican leaders voiced concerns during this meeting about the potential for historic losses.[2] As we now know, these concerns were well-founded as Republicans did indeed suffer significant losses in the House elections. Democrats won a net gain of 40 seats and gained control of the chamber, which led Jacobson (2019a, 9) to contend that the 2018 midterms represented "the most sweeping and discordant national referendum on any administration at least since the Great Depression."

Despite the public focus on electoral accountability in the aftermath of recent midterm elections, the relationship between nationalization and electoral accountability in Congress has received comparatively little attention to date. The implications of nationalization for accountability are insinuated in prior research that notes how the relationship between elected officials and voters may weaken when elections are dominated by top-down considerations (Hopkins 2018; Moskowitz 2021). While these concerns are justified, research on the historical Congress shows that it is possible for congressional candidates to establish an electoral connection with voters in periods of highly nationalized politics (Carson and Engstrom 2005; Carson and Sievert 2018; Finocchiaro and Jenkins 2016). Our primary interest, then, is to explore how electoral accountability operates, if at all, in a more nationalized electoral environment.

While there are reasons to believe that nationalization can make electoral accountability more difficult, we do not believe that it is completely subverted. There are two factors to consider when evaluating how electoral accountability might operate in a more nationalized electoral environment. First, it is important to distinguish between individual and partisan electoral accountability. The former implies that specific *legislators* are rewarded or punished for their actions in office, while the latter implies that a specific *party* is held accountable. While scholars tend to focus more on individual accountability, there are several factors that can impede this form of electoral accountability even in eras of lower nationalization (see, e.g., Carson and Sievert 2018, 127–129). Partisan accountability, however, can be exercised more easily regardless of how nationalized elections become since it merely requires a single party to be rewarded or punished. We observe this type of accountability, for instance, in partisan tides associated with midterm losses for the president's party (Campbell 1985; Kernell 1977a; Oppenheimer, Stimson, and Waterman 1986; Tufte 1975). It is also evident in the type of president-centric economic voting observed recently at most levels of government (Benedictis-Kenner and Warshaw 2020).

Second, it is important to distinguish electoral environments or systems where nationalization is a product of electoral institutions rather than changes in voter behavior (Carson, Sievert, and Williamson 2020). During the 19th century, the electoral institutions, namely the party ballot, required voters to make a choice between parties rather than individual candidates. Under this arrangement, straight-ticket voting was likely to occur by default since voters had little opportunity to split their ticket between candidates of competing parties (Engstrom and Kernell 2005). In the 21st century, by contrast, it is voter behavior—and not institutions—that appears to be driving nationalization (Davis and Mason 2016; Jacobson 2015b; Sievert and McKee 2019). We would therefore expect that the ways in which nationalization would impact electoral accountability may differ across these two periods in American electoral history.

## ELECTION TIMING AND ACCOUNTABILITY IN NATIONALIZED ELECTIONS

During the 19th century, electoral accountability was potentially undermined by the party ballot. Unlike modern electoral ballots, the party ballot listed the slate of candidates of a single party for all offices, which made it difficult (but not impossible) for voters to reward or punish individual politicians (Rusk 1970). In presidential election years, this meant that congressional candidates' electoral fortunes were inexorably tied to their party's presidential candidate when they appeared on the ballot together, thus enhancing the impact of nationalization. Under this arrangement, the conventional view is that attributes of individual congressional candidates should have little impact on election outcomes because candidate-specific factors would be subsumed by national forces (Jacobson 1989). Even in midterm years, the party-centered nature of elections was expected to weaken the role of individual candidates, which in turn would dampen the role of electoral accountability. Both the party ballot and other features of 19th-century elections, such as rotation in office and limited media outlets, would seemingly weaken a strong electoral connection between legislators and their constituents (Bensel 2004; Formisano 1974; Jacobson 1990; Price 1975). Indeed, individual accountability was dramatically enhanced by the adoption of progressive reforms such as the Australian ballot and the direct primary in the late 19th and early 20th centuries (Katz and Sala 1996; Kernell 1977b, 2003; Rusk 1970).

Despite potential institutional barriers to the establishment of an electoral connection in earlier political eras, there is a growing body of literature demonstrating how legislators could indeed be held accountable for their behavior outside of the modern era. In investigating the Compensation Act of 1816, for instance, Bianco, Spence, and Wilkerson (1996) find that electorally vulnerable legislators were less likely to support the unpopular compensation plan and that those who voted in favor of the plan were more likely to retire, forecasting that their support of the pay raise greatly increased the probability of electoral defeat. Additionally, Carson and Engstrom (2005) demonstrate that legislators in the U.S. House who voted for Adams following the disputed presidential election of 1824, but were from districts that supported Jackson, were targeted for defeat and were much more likely to lose in the subsequent midterm elections. More recently, Carson and Sievert (2018) offer a wide range of evidence that legislators were indeed motivated by electoral incentives as far back as the 1820s.[3]

One of the main reasons electoral accountability was possible, at least to a limited degree, is that nationalization was not constant across or even within a given election year. Although congressional candidates' electoral fortunes were tied to presidential candidates in presidential election years because of the electoral institutions, the connection between congressional candidates and the president was weaker during midterm election years (Engstrom and Kernell 2005). The removal of presidential coattails in midterm elections led to less nationalized contests, which meant that the electoral returns of candidate-specific factors increased in these contests (Carson and Sievert 2018). We would therefore expect differences in nationalization *across* election years, which should lead to predictable changes in electoral accountability.

The electoral calendar was also markedly different in this era as states were not yet required to hold their congressional elections on a single day (Engstrom 2012). Since congressional elections were often held on different days from the presidential election throughout much of the 19th century, nationalization was not constant even *within* a single presidential election year. Congressional elections were held over several months, some contests happening months before the November presidential election and others occurring in the subsequent calendar year. The elongated electoral calendar meant that at least some congressional candidates would not appear on the ballot with a presidential candidate. We expect that this should alter the nature of electoral accountability, particularly as it relates to partisan accountability, even within the same electoral cycle.

Based on these two factors, we examine how variation in nationalization, whether because of the type of election or election timing, influenced electoral accountability. To do so, we examine whether two measures—retirements and partisan seat change—varied along with changes in the expected level of nationalization. We believe these two measures provide suitable tests of electoral accountability, and thus the electoral connection, for several reasons. First, individual electoral accountability requires a legislator to seek another term in office, which means that strategically timed retirements can limit voters' ability to punish a given legislator. By contrast, partisan accountability can still be exercised to the extent that the incumbent party suffers electoral losses. Second, in a highly nationalized electoral environment, neither retirements nor partisan seat change should, in theory, vary based on election timing. If top-down forces, such as partisanship and presidential politics, drive vote choice, then the date of an election should not matter.

Given the preceding discussion, we begin our analysis by exploring differences across presidential and midterm elections in 19th-century elections that were highly nationalized because of the party ballot in use. We also investigate differential election timing in promoting greater electoral accountability. From there, we examine congressional retirements in the modern era. We find that legislators were able to establish an electoral connection with voters during both periods of nationalized politics, although there are notable differences considering the distinct electoral rules influencing outcomes in each political era.

## Presidential and Midterm Elections

For our initial examination of the relationship between nationalization and electoral accountability, we calculated the proportion of districts that changed partisan control for both the president's party and the opposition party in presidential and midterm election years.[4] We report these calculations as the gray bars in Figures 4.1a and 4.1b. Since congressional elections were more closely linked with presidential politics during this

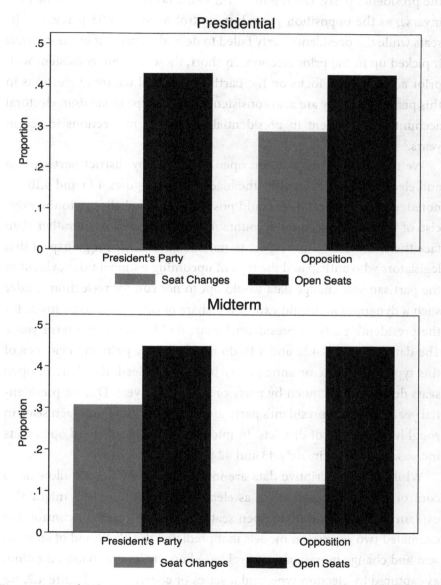

**Figures 4.1a and 4.1b** Partisan Seat Changes and Open-Seat Races by Election Year, 1840–1878

era, it follows that the opposition party should suffer more seat losses in presidential years. Indeed, the president's party lost control of districts it held in just under 13 percent of presidential year races compared with the opposition party, which saw almost 29 percent of its seats being carried by the president's party. During midterm years, however, we found the near inverse, as the opposition party lost control of roughly 13 percent of its seats while the president's party failed to defend 32 percent of the districts it picked up in the prior election. In short, these data are consistent with prior accounts that focus on the partisan-centered nature of elections in this period, but they are also consistent with the type of *partisan* electoral accountability evident in presidential and midterm elections in recent years.[5]

We next turn to the data on open-seat races by district partisanship and election year, depicted by the black bars in Figures 4.1a and 4.1b. As noted, strategic retirements could pose a potential challenge to the exercise of individual electoral accountability if legislators retire rather than face the electorate. With respect to nationalization, we might expect that legislators who anticipated the type of upcoming national tides evident in the partisan seat change data would opt to not run for reelection. Under such a dynamic, we would expect the share of open seats to be lower for the president's party in presidential years and higher in midterm years. The data in Figures 4.1a and 4.1b do not, however, yield any evidence of this type of strategic or anticipatory behavior. Indeed, the share of open seats does not vary much by party or by election year. During presidential years, both the president's party and the opposition had open seats in roughly 40 percent of districts. In midterm years, the share of open seats increased to approximately 43 and 42 percent, respectively.

While these descriptive data are informative, they do not allow us to control for other factors, such as electoral competition, that might also explain the likelihood of an open seat or change in partisan control. We estimated two regression models that predicted the likelihood of an open seat and change in partisan control based on the level of nationalization, as captured by election type, and a series of covariates. In Figure 4.2, we report the marginal effects of membership in the president's party on the

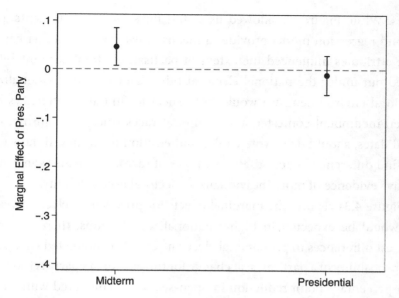

Figure 4.2 Marginal Effects of Shared Partisanship with President on the Probability of an Open-Seat Race by Election Type, 1840–1878

NOTE: The dots denote the estimated marginal effect of partisanship on the probability of an open seat, while the line depicts the 90 percent confidence interval.

probability of an open-seat race by election type. Consistent with the descriptive data in Figures 4.1a and 4.1b, we find no evidence that an open-seat race was common in either party during presidential election years. The estimated marginal effect is near 0 and has a confidence interval that crosses zero. During midterm years, however, we do find that open seats were more common in districts that had been held by the president's party. The marginal effect is small in magnitude, approximately 4 percentage points, but its 90 percent confidence interval does not contain zero. In short, once we account for district-level electoral competition, we do find some modest evidence of strategic retirements among the president's copartisans in years when the national tides were likely to work against them.

For the final aspect of this analysis, we report the results of a logistic regression predicting the probability a district changes partisan control. As before, we compare the effect across election type but focus on the marginal effect of partisanship in incumbent-contested and open-seat races. While Figure 4.2 allowed us to test for strategic retirements, this second regression model provides a means of evaluating whether candidate attributes influenced the extent of partisan electoral accountability doled out under the national electoral tides. Under a fully nationalized electoral environment, we would not expect to find any differences between incumbent-contested and open-seat races since partisanship, not candidates, should drive vote choice and election outcomes. If, however, we find differences across these two types of races, it provides some suggestive evidence of more individualized electoral accountability.

Figure 4.3a reports the marginal effects for presidential election years. As would be expected in highly nationalized elections, there are only modest differences in presidential election years. The predicted change in the probability of a partisan seat change for the president's party is less than a 16-percentage point reduction in open-seat races compared with an 18-point reduction in incumbent-contested races. During midterm election years, however, the pattern reverses, as the predicted chance of a change in partisan control is 17 points in incumbent-contested races compared to a 23-point change in open-seat races (Figure 4.3b). In short, while incumbents from the president's party were punished, they were marginally more likely to hold on to the district than were their counterparts in open seats. While these differences are small, it is still consistent with the pattern one would expect if candidate-specific attributes, such as incumbency or candidate quality, exerted some influence on vote choice and election outcomes. More important for our purposes, these patterns are consistent with the type of behavior one would expect under at least a modest form of *individual* and not just *partisan* electoral accountability.

## Election Timing

While the preceding analysis leverages variation in nationalization across election years, the protracted electoral calendar in the 19th century makes it possible to examine variation in nationalization within the same election year. Specifically, we calculated the rate of partisan seat change and

Nationalization and the Electoral Connection

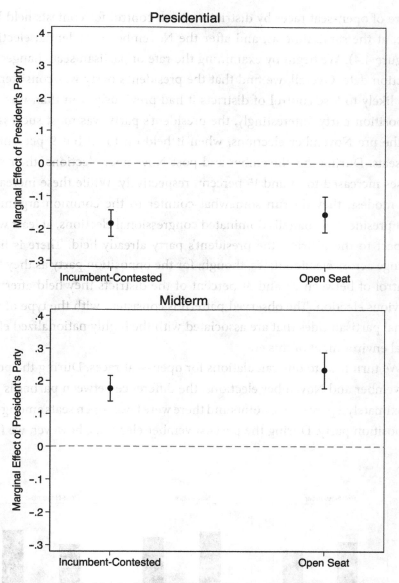

**Figures 4.3a and 4.3b** Marginal Effects of Shared Partisanship with President on the Probability of a Partisan Seat Change by Election Type and Candidate Type, 1840–1878
NOTE: The dots denote the estimated marginal effect of partisanship on the probability of an open seat, while the line depicts the 90 percent confidence interval.

share of open-seat races by district partisan control for contests held before, at the same time as, and after the November presidential election (Figure 4.4). We begin by examining the rate of partisan seat changes by election date. Overall, we find that the president's party was consistently less likely to lose control of districts it had previously won than was the opposition party. Interestingly, the president's party was most successful in the pre-November elections, when it held on to all but 9 percent of its seats. During the November and post-November elections, their seat losses increased to 14 and 15 percent, respectively. While these increases are modest, they do run somewhat counter to the common argument that presidential coattails dominated congressional elections, at least with respect to the districts the president's party already held. There is little change across election dates, though, for the opposition party as they lost control of between 27 and 31 percent of the districts they held after the previous election. The observed pattern is consistent with the type of national partisan tides that are associated with the highly nationalized electoral environment of this era.

We turn next to our calculations for open-seat races. During the post-November and November elections, the difference between parties is approximately 2 percentage points and there were fewer open seats among the opposition party. During the post-November elections, however, we find

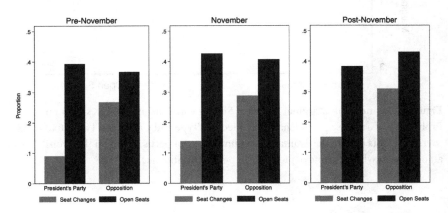

**Figure 4.4** Partisan Seat Changes and Open-Seat Races by Election Date, 1840–1876

a slight reversal with an open-seat race in roughly 38 percent of districts held by the president's party, but there was an open seat in 43 percent of districts controlled by the opposition party. While the difference—5 percentage points—is modest, it is still double the magnitude and constitutes a reversal of the relationship of the two earlier periods. In short, these data provide some evidence of potential strategic retirements, but not necessarily in the anticipated direction.

To examine the relationship more systematically between intrayear nationalization and retirements, we once again estimated a regression model predicting the probability of an open seat across levels of nationalization, as captured by election date, and a series of covariates. In Figure 4.5, we report the marginal effects of membership in the president's party on the probability of an open-seat race by election date. The marginal effects for pre-November and November elections are consistent with the descriptive data in Figure 4.4. Our regression estimates provide no evidence that

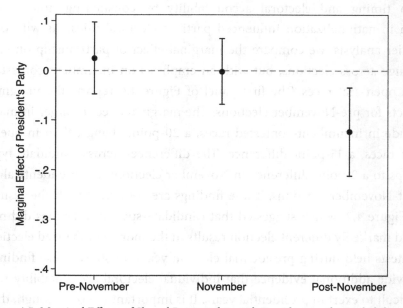

Figure 4.5 Marginal Effects of Shared Partisanship with President on the Probability of an Open-Seat Race by Election Type, 1840–1878
NOTE: The dots denote the estimated marginal effect of partisanship on the probability of an open seat, while the line depicts the 90 percent confidence interval.

an open-seat race was more likely in the two more nationalized periods. For both election dates, the estimated marginal effect is near 0 and has a confidence interval that crosses zero. During post-November elections, however, we do find that open seats were more common in districts that had been held by the opposition party. In these election contests, the change in predicted probability of an open seat was 12 points lower in a district held by the president's party than one held by the opposition party. These results suggest that once we account for electoral competition, we do indeed uncover evidence of strategic retirements. Interestingly, these retirements were more common in what we would expect to be the least nationalized periods in American history. In short, while nationalization may not have influenced retirements per se, there is still evidence that incumbents in the disadvantaged party, namely the opposition party, responded rationally to the partisan tides evidenced in early congressional contests.

We conclude our examination of the relationship between election timing and electoral accountability by considering how variation in nationalization influenced partisan electoral tides. As with our earlier analysis, we compare the marginal effect of partisanship on seat change across elections, but with an emphasis on incumbent-contested and open-seat races. The first panel of Figure 4.6 reports the marginal effects for pre-November elections. The marginal effect is larger in magnitude in incumbent-contested races, a 20-point change, than in open-seat races, a 15-point difference. The differences across candidate type drops to a 2-point difference in November elections and are identical in post-November elections. These findings are consistent with the results in Figure 4.2, which suggested that candidate-specific attributes did not yield markedly different election results in the more nationalized election contests held during presidential election years. In short, these findings provide additional evidence that individual electoral accountability was difficult to exert in presidential years. It is important to note, though, that these results might still be consistent with a form of partisan electoral accountability.

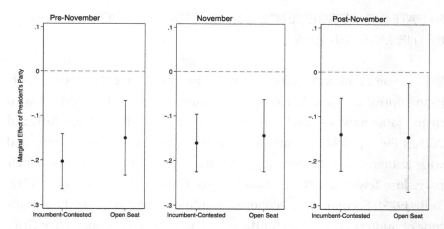

**Figure 4.6** Marginal Effects of Shared Partisanship with President on the Probability of a Partisan Seat Change by Election Date and Candidate Type, 1840–1876
NOTE: The dots denote he estimated marginal effect of partisanship on the probability of an open seat, while the line depicts the 90 percent confidence interval.

In sum, these findings demonstrate that candidate-specific effects were present during the 19th century, when elections were nationalized, although the effects are more pronounced in midterms than in presidential elections. Indeed, our results are consistent with Jacobson's (2015c) argument about nationalization and suggest that his theoretical explanation is applicable to congressional elections across a large swath of American history. It is important to note, however, that there is a crucial difference between the period we examine and modern elections. During the 19th century, nationalized elections were the result of the institutions that governed elections (e.g., the party ballot) rather than voters *choosing* to cast a vote for presidential and congressional candidates of the same party. As such, the structure of the ballot itself makes this period a particularly difficult test case in which to find evidence of candidate-specific effects. The fact that we still find evidence of candidate attributes influencing electoral outcomes during this period suggests that the preconditions for electoral accountability were present, even if in a limited form, during the 19th century.

## STRATEGIC RETIREMENTS AND NATIONALIZATION IN THE MODERN ERA

While recent midterm elections have led to more frequent changes in partisan control of the U.S. House, these outcomes are still largely shaped by the same national-level conditions (see, e.g., Jacobson 2007, 2011, and 2015c). First, public evaluations of the president are positively correlated with midterm seat changes such that more popular presidents see their party lose fewer seats (Abramowitz 1985; Campbell 1985; Kernell 1977a; Tufte 1975). Second, poor economic conditions may increase the magnitude of midterm seat losses for the president's party (Campbell 1985; Grier and McGarrity 2002; Lynch 2002; Tufte 1975). Third, if the president's party is overexposed in Congress, which is determined by the extent to which a party has more seats than its long-term norm, the party becomes particularly vulnerable in the next election (Oppenheimer, Stimson, and Waterman 1986; Jacobson 2011).

While the "fundamentals" of modern midterm elections are not always discussed in conjunction with strategic retirements, they are clearly related. According to strategic politician theory (Jacobson and Kernell 1983), macro-level conditions, such as presidential approval and economic conditions, are translated into election outcomes by the decisions of political elites. While previous research largely conceptualizes the decision of political elites in terms of challenger entry decisions (Jacobson 1989; Jacobson and Kernell 1983), incumbent legislators are no less strategic than their potential challengers. As with the decision to run for office in the first place, incumbent career decisions can be understood in terms of a strategic calculation (Carson 2005). Indeed, existing work generally relies upon a similar theoretical foundation and assumes that retirements are "the result of an evaluation of the relative costs and benefits of House service" (Brace 1985, 108). The potential costs of running can include both electoral considerations (Brace 1985; Hibbing and Alford 1981; Fulton et al. 2006), intra-institutional ambition and position (Carson 2005; Hall and van Houweling 1995; Kiewit and Zeng 1993), and financial interests (Brace 1985; Groseclose and Krehbiel 1994; Hall and van Houweling 1995).

What precisely influences these calculations does, however, vary across related work. For example, some research finds that an incumbent's prior electoral margin has little, or at best mixed, effect on retirement decisions (Brace 1985; Carson 2005; Hall and van Houweling 1995; Kiewit and Zeng 1993). Other scholars report that perceptions or beliefs about future electoral prospects can influence career decisions (Hibbing 1982a, 1982b; Maestas et al. 2006). Based on interviews with retired representatives, Hibbing (1982b, 64) concluded that although electoral concerns alone may not be able to explain all retirements, "they are an important and frequently mentioned cost of serving in the House." Incumbents' concern about the prospect of a difficult reelection may help to explain why scandals and redistricting lead incumbents to retire at higher rates (Brace 1985; Carson 2005).

Incumbents' sensitivity to their own potential electoral vulnerability suggests why it is theoretically important to consider how strategic retirements might influence midterm losses. However, a potential connection between midterms and strategic retirements may not be felt symmetrically between the two parties. Research on the post–World War II era finds that Republican incumbents voluntarily retire from the House at a higher rate than their Democratic counterparts (Ang and Overby 2008; Gilmour and Rothstein 1993). Gilmour and Rothstein (1993) were originally interested in partisan differences in retirements as a potential cause of Democratic dominance in the House. In a follow-up study, Ang and Overby (2008) found that this trend persisted even after Republicans regained control of the House majority. An important implication of this partisan difference is that retirements should have a greater impact on Republican midterm losses than for Democrats in the modern era.

The rise of more nationalized elections could indicate that retirements have little systematic impact on midterm losses. If partisanship rather than candidate-level factors primarily governs election outcomes, then the presence or absence of an incumbent should not influence partisan control of a district as it once did. The potential returns of incumbency were a key theoretical component of Gilmour and Rothstein's (1993, 346) argument: "Unless incumbents have an advantage in running for a congressional seat, differences between parties in their retirement rates will have no impact on partisan balance." If the once robust incumbency advantage has been eroded in recent elections, it should be difficult, if not impossible, to find any relationship between retirements and midterm losses.

Given the preceding discussion, we have several clear expectations related to the impact of increased nationalization on turnover in recent midterm elections. The first pertains to the electoral fortunes of members of the president's party. Considering how presidents generally see their popularity decline throughout their tenure and the historical trend of losing seats in midterm elections, strategic incumbents are inclined to voluntarily leave office rather than risk a tough reelection battle that may ultimately result in their defeat. Therefore, we expect the president's party to see more members retire in midterm elections.

Second, retirements should have an asymmetric effect on congressional elections across parties. As previously mentioned, Republicans tend to retire at higher rates than Democrats. The GOP has also imposed term limits on its committee chairs in recent years while consolidating power in the hands of the House Speaker by eliminating earmarks and increasingly relying on closed rules when considering legislation. Therefore, being relegated from a committee chair to a relatively powerless rank-and-file member may not be especially appealing to many legislators (Reynolds 2017). As Jacobson (2015a) demonstrates, however, Republicans enjoy a structural advantage in House elections. Their voters are more efficiently distributed across congressional districts relative to Democrats', making many of their incumbents electorally safer even under adverse partisan tides. As such, we should expect Republican seat losses to be more likely caused by incumbents voluntarily leaving office, whereas Democratic seat losses should more likely be caused by incumbents losing reelection (i.e., involuntary departures).

Third, an increase in the nationalization of elections means that voters tend to place a greater emphasis on which party they would like to control government instead of selecting between candidates based on their individual characteristics. The primary determinant of vote choice thus should be the partisanship of the candidate, which translates into little to no effect on other factors—namely incumbency. We would therefore expect incumbent retirements to have no impact on midterm losses in this more nationalized political environment.

To test these theoretical expectations, we begin by examining descriptive trends in U.S. House elections over a longer time series. The top panel of Figure 4.7 displays the number of retirements for members of either party between 1954 and 2020 using data from *Vital Statistics on Congress* or official elections returns. The average number of retirements for Democratic members is 15.8, while the same figure for Republicans is 18.2. In the 34 election cycles examined here, Republicans retired in greater numbers than Democrats 19 times and at equal numbers twice. There were only 13 election years in which Democratic retirements exceeded Republican. These patterns conform to previous findings even considering the evolving electoral landscape.

The other panels of Figure 4.7 shows the same relationship, this time separated by the president's party and the party out of power as well as separated by presidential and midterm elections. On average, the president's party witnessed 18.8 members retire from the House, whereas only 15.3 members of the opposition elected to do so. This discrepancy increased when looking only at midterm elections. Nearly 20 (19.9) members of the president's party retired, on average, while only 14.4 members of the opposition party did so. Indeed, members of the president's party retired at higher rates than members of the opposition party in 13 of the 17 midterm election years observed here. The difference is relatively negligible in presidential election years, as almost 18 House members from the president's party retired compared to just 16 of their opposition party counterparts. Collectively, these figures provide preliminary evidence in support of the idea that irrespective of time or partisanship, members of the president's party retire at higher rates during midterm elections than do members of the party out of power, which suggests some tangible fear of electoral retribution.

Although Democrats and Republicans retire at different rates, a raw count reveals no discernible difference and considerable symmetry in the number of incumbent defeats and open-seat losses. However, it is important to keep in mind that Democrats controlled greater shares of seats during this era. On average, the Democratic Party held 240 seats,

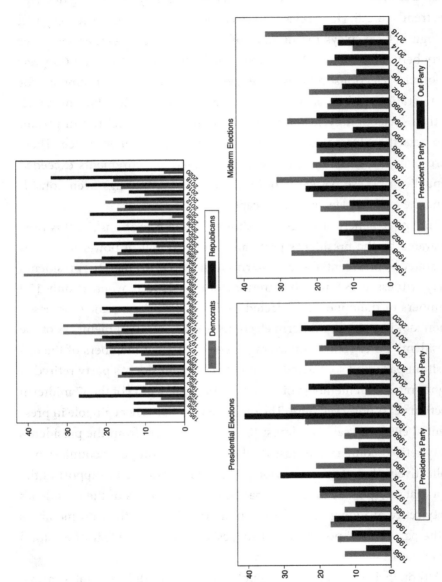

**Figure 4.7** Number of House Retirements by Party, 1954–2020

while the Republicans held only 194. The previously mentioned similar numbers are greater in magnitude for the GOP. Incumbent reelection rates generally exceed 90 percent (Jacobson and Carson 2020), but 3.8 percent of Democratic incumbents lose on average, while 5.1 percent of Republicans do so.

Descriptively, we find that in-party members voluntarily exit office more than out-party members during midterms, but the relationship is a bit more nuanced. Retirements are increasingly less common overall and asymmetric across parties, especially in more recent years. Therefore, we believe it is important to consider the level of nationalization and the partisanship of the controlling party when analyzing seat changes in Congress. To systematically examine this dynamic, we predict partisan seat change by candidate type in both presidential and midterm elections in two different 10-year periods in the modern era. The first era consists of elections from 1968 to 1978, and the second consists of elections from 2008 to 2018. Figure 4.8 depicts the differences in presidential election years between these two time periods. We find that shared partisanship with the president does not have a predictable effect on seat changes in Congress for incumbent-contested races as well as open seats in either era.

We find a markedly different pattern when we examine midterm elections. In Figure 4.9, all four models predict that being affiliated with

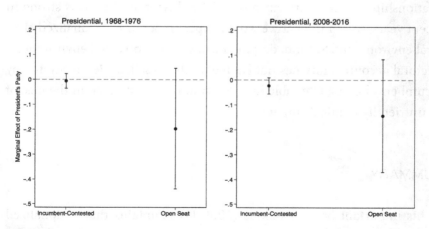

**Figure 4.8** Partisan Seat Changes by Candidate Type in Presidential Elections
NOTE: The dots denote the estimated marginal effect of partisanship on the probability of an open seat, while the line depicts the 90 percent confidence interval.

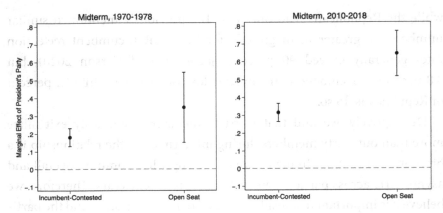

**Figure 4.9** Partisan Seat Changes by Candidate Type in Midterm Elections
NOTE: The dots denote the estimated marginal effect of partisanship on the probability of an open seat, while the line depicts the 90 percent confidence interval.

the president's party increases the probability of a seat changing partisan hands. During the 1970s, however, the coefficient is relatively small in magnitude (0.18 for incumbent-contested races and 0.35 for open seats), and there is comparatively more uncertainty in the estimate for open-seat races. In the more recent elections, the magnitude of the effect is greater and the effect is stronger in open seats than for incumbent-contested elections (0.32 for incumbent-contested races and 0.64 for open seats). Taken collectively, Figures 4.8 and 4.9 lead us to two specific conclusions. First, the relationship between partisanship and seat loss in midterms is strong in recent years, which is what we would expect in a more nationalized electoral environment. Second, despite this highly nationalized environment, electoral accountability has not been entirely erased, as demonstrated by incumbents being better able to hold on to their seats even in the face of an unfriendly political climate.

## SUMMARY

In his important book, Hopkins (2018, 19) maintains that nationalized "voting patterns have the potential to dampen the electoral connection between voters and officials, as state and local officials may come to believe they are insulated from the threat of losing at the ballot box." In this chapter, we have sought to investigate this claim more systematically across congressional elections from two different eras. In the first part of the chapter, we show that it is possible for congressional candidates to establish an electoral connection with voters even during a highly nationalized era of politics. Prior to the early 1880s, presidential and congressional elections were not consistently held on the same day. Indeed, as many as two-thirds of congressional elections during this era occurred on a different date than the presidential election. This means that the candidate for the U.S. House seat was likely to be at the top of the party ballot, which enabled him to cultivate a personal vote even in this highly nationalized era. This is exactly what we find in our analysis of strategic retirements in 19th-century congressional elections.

We also examined the incidence of congressional retirements in elections held during the post–World War II era to speak to the effects of the more recent pattern of nationalized elections. Based on our analysis, we find greater parity between the two parties when it comes to incumbent retirements. Whereas Republican losses had primarily been driven by open-seat losses and Democratic losses stemmed more from incumbent defeats previously, that pattern no longer appears to be the case in the more recent, nationalized elections. This suggests that legislative retirements do not have as pronounced effect on the number of seat losses given the declining value of incumbency in Congress. Thus, even though nationalization has been on the rise, there still appears to be room for candidate-specific effects to matter as a greater number of open seats are now likely to change partisan control in a particular election year. Given this dynamic, in the next chapter we delve more deeply into the relationship between nationalization and incumbency over time. Later, we investigate which factors can influence election outcomes during eras of increased nationalization.

# 5

# Nationalization and Incumbency

While the 2016 presidential election was historic and will be discussed and analyzed for years to come, the U.S. House elections played out in a far less dramatic manner. The Republicans suffered a net loss of six seats but still retained a sizable majority thanks in part to seat gains in the 2010 and 2014 midterm elections. The maintenance of the partisan status quo in most districts meant partisan control changed hands in only 12 congressional districts, which was the third-lowest level of partisan turnover in the post–World War II era (Jacobson 2017, 26). These high levels of partisan stability were, in no small part, a reflection of the greater correspondence between the presidential and congressional election results. Whether measured in terms of vote share, vote choice, or election outcomes, the partisan congruence between presidential and congressional elections was more pronounced in 2016 than in any proceeding modern presidential election (Amlani and Algara 2021; Jacobson and Carson 2020; Carson, Sievert, and Williamson 2020; Sievert and McKee 2019).[1]

One important but sometimes overlooked criterion for this type of coattail effect in modern elections is that voters must have the ability to choose a candidate that aligns with their presidential vote choice. Although congressional candidates are strategic and typically identify districts to run in for which they will be competitive, there are still missed opportunities in most election years. In 2016, the Texas 32nd congressional district was the most prominent example of a potential change in partisan control that failed to materialize. The Republican incumbent, Representative Pete

Sessions, faced no Democratic opponent in his bid for an 11th term in office, which was notable because the Democratic presidential nominee, former senator and secretary of state Hillary Clinton, won more votes in the district than Donald Trump in the presidential contest. While Sessions may have been able to retain his seat either way, his ability to discourage a Democratic challenger from even contesting the race thwarted any hopes of Democratic gains.

By the start of the 2018 election cycle, it was clear that Democrats had Sessions at the top of their list for potential pickups. When asked about the potential for a Democratic challenger, Sessions said the 2018 contest would "be a race about whether you're for Nancy Pelosi and big government or whether you're for Republicans to bring things back home. So we'll see what they come up with. Good luck."[2] After failing to run a candidate in 2016, the Democratic primary included seven candidates, and Colin Allred, a former NFL player turned civil rights attorney, was selected as the party's nominee. With both candidates receiving campaign and fundraising assistance from prominent national politicians,[3] the contest became a "microcosm of the House races across the country ... the kind of suburban district Democrats are trying to flip in the Trump era."[4] Ultimately, the combination of a well-funded challenger and a Democratic midterm wave proved to be too much for Sessions to weather, and Allred carried the district by a 6-point margin. The dramatic reversal in Sessions's electoral fortunes between 2016 and 2018 leads us to the overarching question of this chapter: What is the value of incumbency in a highly nationalized electoral environment?

## INCUMBENCY ADVANTAGE IN CONGRESS

Robert Michel (R-IL) represented Illinois's 18th district in the U.S. House of Representatives from January 3, 1957, through January 3, 1995—nearly four decades of service. He served as the House minority whip from 1975 through 1981 and the House minority leader for the Republicans from 1981 until he retired. During his time in office, the Democrats controlled a majority of the seats in the chamber, which prevented him from having the chance to serve as the Speaker during his long career. Upon Michel's retirement, Newt Gingrich became the Speaker of the House after the Republicans captured control of the chamber following 40 years of Democratic dominance.

Michel's career is emblematic of the "textbook Congress," where he served for a time as a rank-and-file member, worked his way into the leadership, and retired at the age of 72. Michel was well known for his bipartisanship in Congress and his ability to work across the aisle with Democrats such as Speaker "Tip" O'Neill and Dan Rostenkowski, long-time chair of the Ways and Means Committee. Before getting elected to the House in the 1956 election, Michel worked as an administrative assistant to U.S. House member Harold Velde from 1949 to 1956, where he grew to appreciate the inner workings of the chamber and the importance of working with both parties on key pieces of legislation, such as the Civil Rights Acts of 1957, 1964, and 1968 as well as the Voting Rights Act of 1965. He received an average of 61.6 percent of the vote in the 19 House elections in which he was a candidate, including one race in which he ran unopposed. His vote share dipped below 54 percent only once, despite the state being relatively competitive at the presidential level during his tenure and other House seats changing hands around him.

Since the early 1970s, students of congressional elections have systematically investigated the incidence and growth of the incumbency advantage in Congress, like that afforded to Michel. In fact, more attention has been given to this subject in the congressional elections literature than nearly any other topic to date. What began as a relatively simple endeavor to identify why incumbents tend to win more often than their challengers (see, e.g., Erikson 1971; Mayhew 1974a) has steadily evolved into a series of more complex arguments that typically involve what incumbents are doing well (see, e.g., Gelman and King 1990; Cox and Katz 1996) rather than what challengers are doing poorly or not at all (Hinckley 1980; Jacobson and Kernell 1983). More recently, analyses of the incumbency advantage have employed sophisticated methodological innovations (Ansolabehere, Snyder, and Stewart 2000; Erikson and Titiunik 2015;

Fouirnaies and Hall 2014) to gain leverage on this important question. At the same time, other scholars have argued that the incumbency advantage has declined (Jacobson 2015b) or is merely a statistical artifact that results from how scholars operationalize their empirical analyses (Stonecash 2008). Our analysis builds on this classic body of work that has important implications for representation and finds that incumbents have been advantaged over their challengers since at least the early 19th century. The size of this benefit, however, fluctuates in predictable ways over time with respect to how nationalized the elections are.

Although much has been written during the past 50 years about the advantages accruing to incumbents, a variety of unanswered questions remain. For instance, we still do not have a firm understanding of the underlying factors that have contributed to the high reelection rate for incumbents during the modern era. Is it a function of advantages that naturally accrue to legislators (i.e., casework, position-taking, or credit claiming), or can it be better explained by shortcomings of the challengers (limited resources or inexperience) that incumbents usually face? Furthermore, do current theories about the incumbency advantage help to systematically explain historical variability in incumbent electoral success? Or do we need to modify our theories to account for different institutional arrangements and political circumstances across a broader period of history?

To answer these questions, we first must revisit some of the most prominent literature from Chapter 2. Students of elections as well as casual observers of American politics routinely note that incumbent members of Congress retain their positions irrespective of factors that would seem to threaten their job security. Even when faced with low institutional approval, a seeming inability to enact meaningful legislation, and strong partisan tides, it is not uncommon for Americans to return approximately 90 percent of representatives to their offices. As such, members often win reelection despite these extenuating circumstances. The ability of incumbents to outperform these circumstances has arguably spurred more discussion within the congressional elections literature than any other issue.

Congressional scholars began investigating the possible advantages of incumbency as far back as the early 1970s (see, e.g., Erikson 1971; Mayhew 1974b; Ferejohn 1977; Cover 1977; Fiorina 1977). Trying to identify the factors responsible for cultivating this electoral phenomenon, they found institutional features such as legislative casework (Fiorina 1977), legislative activism (Johannes and McAdams 1981), advertising (Cover and Brumberg 1982), replacement among members (Born 1979; Alford and Hibbing 1981), and redistricting (Erikson 1972; Cover 1977).[5] Others argued that behavioral explanations were more appropriate. For example, some believe that the advantage can be explained by legislators' personal home styles in their district (Fenno 1978), rational entry and exit decisions by strategic candidates (Jacobson and Kernell 1983; Krasno 1994; Cox and Katz 1996), a growing "personal" vote (Cain, Ferejohn, and Fiorina 1987), a greater emphasis on television appearances in a candidate-centered electoral era (Prior 2007), or better ideological posturing relative to their challengers (Carson and Williamson 2018b).[6]

Still other works place considerable weight on the role of donations and money. Both House and Senate campaigns have become more costly over time (Abramowitz 1989, 1991), a disproportionate amount of that money being raised and spent by incumbents (i.e., the "strategic money" thesis discussed by Jacobson and Kernell 1983; see also Herrnson 2012 for more evidence on this point). Box-Steffensmeier (1996) demonstrates that incumbents do not necessarily have to outspend their opponents, but instead can simply scare off potentially strong challengers by amassing large war chests.

## INCUMBENCY IN HISTORICAL CONTEXT

While the bulk of research on the incumbency advantage focuses on the period from the 1960s onward, prior research suggests evidence of an incumbency advantage in earlier periods. Garand and Gross (1984) and Gross and Garand (1984) report evidence of an upward trend in incumbent electoral security as far back as the 1890s. More intriguing, Garand

and Gross (1984, 29) find that "incumbent winners have always done better than non-incumbent winners," but the magnitude of the incumbency advantage, as captured by vote margins, began to increase in the 1890s. In Figure 5.1 the black line depicts the proportion of U.S. House incumbents deciding to run for reelection from 1840 to 2020. These numbers are considerably lower in the first six decades of the time series but reached levels comparable to the modern age around the turn of the century. The 1848 and 1850 elections are the only two elections in which fewer than half of eligible incumbents sought reelection. Fewer than 55 percent of incumbents ran again in 1846 and 1860, but these are the only four years with such high turnover. Though the House was welcoming larger numbers of freshman during this time, the modal election still featured an incumbent candidate. Since 1900, an average of 87.2 percent of incumbents were seeking another term in office, with over 90 percent running again in 24 election cycles.

While there is variability in the share of incumbents who sought another term, the rate at which those incumbents who do run and win

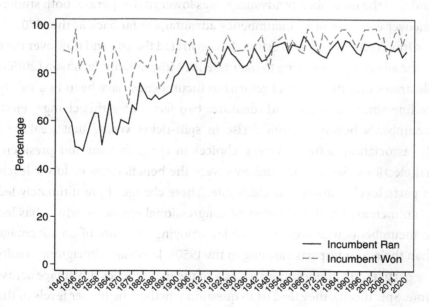

**Figure 5.1** Proportion of Incumbents Seeking and Winning Reelection, 1840–2020

has remained comparatively stable across time. The dashed gray line represents the proportion of incumbents who successfully won reelection over the entire time series. In our entire 180-year time series, only six election cycles bore witness to fewer than 75 percent of incumbents maintaining their seat in the House of Representatives. The least successful year for incumbents came in 1842, when only 65 percent of those seeking reelection accomplished their goal. For all races between 1840 and 2020, 90.5 percent of all House members seeking reelection managed to do so. This demonstrates that an incumbency advantage in some form has existed prior to high polarization, record levels of fundraising and spending, technological advances such as radio and television, or even the rise of candidate-centered races.

While the descriptive evidence reported in Figure 5.1 indicates that incumbents have always won reelection at high rates, more recent studies have reported more direct estimates of the incumbency advantage from the 1870s to the mid-20th century. Carson, Engstrom, and Roberts (2007) and Carson and Roberts (2013) employ the Cox-Katz measure to estimate the incumbency advantage in these historical elections. Although they find that the incumbency advantage was lower in this period, both studies uncover evidence of an incumbency advantage as far back as the 1870s.

Other recent work has further demonstrated the ebb and flow over time in the advantages accruing to incumbents. Most notably, Jacobson (2015b) illustrates that the electoral returns to incumbency have been in a steady decline since the 1980s and identifies two factors for this change. First, incumbents benefited from a rise in split-ticket voting that weakened the association between voters' choices in congressional and presidential elections. Second, incumbents were the beneficiaries of lower levels of party loyalty among the electorate. These changes have ultimately led to an increased nationalization of congressional elections, which has led to incumbents who seek office today enjoying no more of an advantage than their counterparts running in the 1950s. Jacobson's intriguing results are particularly important for a study of the incumbency advantage across time. Specifically, they lead us to question whether the higher levels of the incumbency advantage between the 1960s and early 2000s are anomalous to a larger time frame. Building off this work, as well as the work of Carson, Sievert, and Williamson (2020), the remainder of this chapter maps this trend and assesses the most appropriate means by which to evaluate it.

## NATIONALIZATION AND THE INCUMBENCY ADVANTAGE OVER TIME

Jacobson's (2015b) findings and conclusions are especially noteworthy for an analysis of the incumbency advantage across different political eras. As discussed in earlier chapters, the electoral institutions in place throughout the mid- to late 19th century led to exactly the type of party-oriented or top-down electoral process that is the hallmark of nationalized elections. The use of the party ballot resulted in a greater level of nationalization since the ballot organized voters' choices by party rather than simply as a collection of individual candidates (Engstrom and Kernell 2005, 2014). Despite the high levels of nationalization throughout the 19th century, there is considerable evidence that attributes of both individual candidates and incumbency structured congressional election outcomes during this period (Carson and Roberts 2013; Carson and Sievert 2017, 2018; Garand and Gross 1984; Gross and Garand 1984). Although the advantage accruing to incumbents was smaller in magnitude during this period, prior research finds evidence that one still existed as far back as the early 1870s (Carson and Roberts 2013).

If nationalization influences the rise and fall of the incumbency advantage, what are we to make of evidence of the latter's existence during a period of highly nationalized elections? We contend that the answer is, at least in part, that it may not be possible to fully erode the advantages of incumbency. As depicted in Figure 5.1, most House incumbents who ran for reelection secured another term in office. Furthermore, Carson and Sievert's (2017) analysis of elections from the party ballot era finds that although the effect of candidate quality was significant in both presidential and midterm election years, it was notably larger in the latter. As such, they conclude that while "nationalization weakens the effect of candidate-specific factors, individual candidates can still influence election outcomes during periods of highly nationalized elections where party line voting is pervasive" (542).

It is of course important to acknowledge that there are substantive differences between nationalization in the 19th century and today, as outlined in earlier chapters. The differences stemming from increased nationalization under the party ballot versus voter choice have important consequences as it means that contemporary congressional voters are still able to divide their support among parties, even if fewer of them choose to do so. For example, very few congressional incumbents in 2016 represented districts won by the other party's presidential candidate, but those who did still won reelection at surprisingly high rates (Jacobson 2017, 28). Such an outcome would have been extremely unlikely under the party ballot in cases where the presidential and congressional candidates appeared on the same ballot.

Based on these considerations, we posit that nationalization can assist us in explaining fluctuations in the effect of incumbency over time. To be clear, we are not suggesting that other factors cannot strengthen or weaken the incumbency advantage or even undermine the effect of nationalization in specific instances. Our argument is rather that nationalization establishes a baseline for the potential electoral effects of incumbency. We therefore expect that the direct, or candidate-specific, effect of incumbency (Cox and Katz 1996; Erikson and Titiunik 2015) should be greatest in periods of low nationalization. Other factors, such as a scare-off effect (Cox and Katz 1996), may remain relevant even in periods of highly nationalized elections if potential challengers are still strategic about when and where they decide to run (Jacobson and Kernell 1983; Rogers 2016).[7] Indeed, this expectation comports with the growing evidence of candidate-specific effects in elections during the more nationalized period of the mid- to late 19th century (Carson and Roberts 2013; Carson and Sievert 2017). If nationalization is an important driver of the incumbency advantage, it should also follow that the higher levels of the advantage observed between the 1960s and the 1990s are anomalous when viewed in a larger time frame.

In sum, we theorize that even as far back as the 1840s, representatives seeking to return to Congress had the opportunity to accrue certain benefits that made them more likely to win their reelection bids (see, e.g., Engstrom 2012; Finocchiaro and MacKenzie 2018). We also maintain that this incumbency advantage can increase in eras of low nationalization but will decrease when nationalization rises, as we have seen during recent decades. Furthermore, we argue that nationalization can have distinct causes at different times in history. Between 1840 and 2020, for instance, nationalization may be a product of either institutional features (i.e., the party ballot in use during the 19th century) or extra-institutional features (i.e., polarization and more uniform voter preferences). The dampening effect of nationalization on the *overall* incumbency advantage will appear largely the same regardless of the underlying cause.

## MEASURING THE INCUMBENCY ADVANTAGE

Beginning in the 1990s, scholars seeking to account for the incumbency advantage began to develop more rigorous and sophisticated measurements of this phenomenon. Gelman and King (1990), for instance, demonstrate that common measures of the incumbency advantage (e.g., the sophomore surge, the retirement slump) are biased and/or inconsistent since they are based on a relatively small sample of legislative races in a given election year. They propose a regression-based estimator that avoids this type of problem.[8] Cox and Katz (1996) later proposed a second regression-based estimator that built on Gelman and King's earlier theoretical and methodological foundations. While a detailed discussion of either set of scholars' empirical and theoretical argument is beyond the scope of this chapter, we do want to briefly review their respective models. Gelman and King's (1990) outcome variable is the Democratic share of the two-party vote (Dem. Vote$_{it}$) in the most recent election. The key predictor captures incumbency status (Incumbent$_{it}$) in each race and is coded 1 if a Democratic incumbent runs for reelection, 0 if no incumbent runs, and −1 if a non-Democratic incumbent runs. Gelman and King's regression model includes two additional control variables. The first control is the lagged Democratic share of the two-party vote (Dem. Vote$_{it-1}$), and the second is an indicator variable (Party$_{it}$) that accounts for which party won the election in each district. It is coded 1 if the Democratic candidate wins the election and −1 if the non-Democratic candidate wins. This model is presented in Equation 5.1, where the estimate for $\theta$ captures the effect of incumbency.

$$\text{Dem. Vote}_{it} = \beta_0 + \beta_1 \text{ Dem. Vote}_{it-1} + \beta_1 \text{ Party}_{it} + \theta \text{ Incumbent}_{it} + \epsilon_{it} \quad (5.1)$$

Cox and Katz (1996) extended the Gelman-King measure by arguing that the incumbency advantage is composed of both a direct and an indirect effect. The direct effect is simply the "perks" associated with being an incumbent (e.g., resources, constituency service), while the indirect effect can be thought of as the ability to deter high-quality challengers from entering the election. They further break down the indirect component into a quality effect, which is analogous to Jacobson's (1989) candidate quality effect, and a scare-off effect, which captures the ability of incumbents to deter higher-quality challengers from running against them (with substantial war chests, for example). Cox and Katz posit that the dramatic growth in the incumbency advantage during the second half of the 20th century was a product of an increase in the quality effect.

To model both direct and indirect components, Cox and Katz present two separate regression models. The outcome variable in the first model is the Democratic share of the two-party vote, and the measure of incumbency remains the same as in the Gelman and King model. Cox and Katz do, however, include two additional control variables. The first is a measure of lagged incumbency (Incumbent$_{it-1}$); the second measure controls for candidate quality in current and past elections (DQA$_{it}$ and DQA$_{it-1}$). The latter measures are coded 1 if the Democratic candidate is the only one who previously held an elected office, 0 if neither candidate has previously held an elected position, and −1 when a non-Democratic candidate is the only one who previously held an elected office. As before, the estimate for $\theta$ captures the direct effect of incumbency and the estimate for $\rho$ denotes the "quality" effect (Equation 5.2).

$$\text{Dem. Vote}_{it} = \beta_0 + \beta_1 \text{Dem. Vote}_{it-1} + \beta_2 \text{Party}_{it} + \theta \text{Incumbent}_{it}$$
$$+ B_3 \text{Incumbent}_{it-1} + \rho \text{DQA}_{it} + \beta_5 \text{DQA}_{it-1} + \epsilon_{it} \quad (5.2)$$

$$\text{DQA}_{it} = \gamma_0 + \gamma_1 \text{Dem. Vote}_{it-1} + \gamma_2 \text{Party}_{it} + \delta \text{Incumbent}_{it}$$
$$+ \gamma_3 \text{Incumbent}_{it-1} + \gamma_5 \text{DQA}_{it-1} + \upsilon_{it} \quad (5.3)$$

In the second regression model, shown in Equation 5.3, the outcome variable, $\text{DQA}_{it}$, measures the candidate quality advantage in a given race. The predictors are largely the same, but now the estimate for the incumbency measure is said to represent the "scare-off" effect of having an incumbent in the race. Cox and Katz calculate the indirect incumbency advantage by multiplying the coefficient estimates for the quality effect from the first regression model and the coefficient estimate for the scare-off effect in the second regression model. The overall incumbency advantage is then calculated by adding the direct and indirect effect ($\theta + \rho\delta$).

To estimate each of these canonical measures of the incumbency advantage, we needed to identify two key pieces of information for each congressional election from 1840 to 2020. First, we need to know the names and partisan affiliation of the candidates in each congressional race to determine if the contest featured an incumbent or was an open-seat race. For elections from 1946 to present, we utilize Jacobson and Carson's (2020) database on congressional candidates, while the candidate and vote returns data for elections before 1946 were collected from Dubin's (1998) *United States Congressional Elections, 1788–1997*, the most comprehensive source for historical election returns. Second, since candidate quality plays an important role in the Cox and Katz estimates of the incumbency advantage, it was also necessary to collect data on candidates' political backgrounds. Our data on candidate quality in congressional elections since 1946 come from Jacobson and Carson (2020), and our data for the period from 1840 to 1944 come from Carson and Roberts (2013) and Carson and Sievert (2018).[9]

The most recent methodological development is the use of the regression discontinuity design (RDD) to measure the incumbency advantage in House elections (Erikson and Titiunik 2015; Lee 2008). Regression discontinuity exploits the "as if" random assignment of winners and losers in close elections to obtain an estimate of the electoral returns to incumbency.[10] Although there is an ongoing debate about whether House elections satisfy key empirical assumptions that underlie the RDD (see Caughey and Sekhon 2011; de la Cuesta and Imai 2016; Erikson and Rader 2017; Eggers et al. 2015), there is an additional consideration that must be taken into account. Most studies define incumbency in terms of the incumbent *party* (i.e., the party that won the prior election) rather than the incumbent *legislator* (Erikson and Titiunik 2015). As a result, the regression discontinuity estimates reported in most studies capture the advantage for the incumbent *party* rather than only the incumbent *legislators*.

Erikson and Titiunik (2015, 103) note that the personal incumbency advantage is the "quantity that has long been of interest to substantive scholars," which points to a potential roadblock in the application of this new method. These authors therefore outline an estimation strategy that focuses on the subset of first-term incumbents who entered office by winning an open-seat election that can be used to measure the personal incumbency advantage. According to Erikson and Titiunik, this subset of legislators is ideal because

> the vote share in the following election reflects two changes—the officeholding premium from incumbency status (the direct personal incumbency advantage), plus any decline in challenger quality that arises from the incumbent's deterring ability (the indirect scareoff effect). At the RD cutoff, the arbitrary winner has no net advantage due to greater candidate quality (vote appeal) or quality-induced scareoff. (105)

The modeling strategy therefore sacrifices generalizability in order to obtain an RDD-based estimate of the personal incumbency advantage.

## Incumbency Advantage across Time

By examining each of these empirical models across a longer time span than is normally considered, we are able not only to assess the robustness of our findings but also to provide a better understanding of the dynamics underlying the relationship between nationalization and incumbency. We begin by examining the Gelman-King and Cox-Katz estimates of the incumbency advantage for the entire period under study.[11] In Figure 5.2, we report the overall estimate of the incumbency advantage for both estimators. The solid gray line denotes the estimate for the Gelman-King model, and the dashed black line reports the calculation based on the Cox-Katz estimator. These regression-based approaches produce effectively identical results across the entire 180-year period and are correlated at 0.99. As with other studies, these estimates capture the dramatic increase in the incumbency advantage in the 1960s. In the 1950s, the incumbency advantage was never greater than 4 percentage points, but the estimate is more than double that in most elections in the 1960s through the 1990s. The results reported in Figure 5.2 also capture the decline in

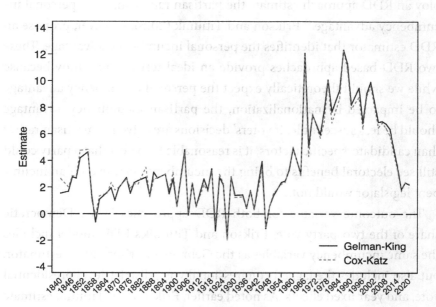

Figure 5.2 Comparison of Gelman-King and Cox-Katz Measures by Year

the incumbency advantage throughout more recent elections (Jacobson 2015b).[12]

Of more immediate interest for our purposes, however, are the estimates for the 19th century. Contrary to the expectations of research that views the incumbency advantage as a strictly modern phenomenon, the estimates of the incumbency advantage were higher throughout much of this period than during the early 20th century. During the 1840s, for instance, the incumbency advantage was around 2 to 3 percentage points, which is slightly higher than that observed in 2018 or 2020, when elections were highly nationalized. Throughout the late 1850s and 1860s, however, the incumbency advantage was notably lower. The decrease in the 1850s and 1860s makes sense since during this period the intersectional politics that defined the Democratic-Whig divisions slowly gave way to more regionally defined party bases (Aldrich 2010). Further still, the estimates throughout the 1870s and 1880s are often higher than those in the early decades of the 20th century since this period established the conditions for more candidate-centered election campaigns (Reynolds 2006; Ware 2002).

As we noted above, many studies of the incumbency advantage that employ an RDD approach estimate the partisan rather than the personal incumbency advantage.[13] Erikson and Titiunik (2015), however, propose an RDD estimator that identifies the personal incumbency advantage. These two RDD-based approaches provide an ideal test for our study because while we should theoretically expect the personal incumbency advantage to be impacted by nationalization, the partisan incumbency advantage should be less susceptible. If voters' decisions are driven by partisan rather than candidate-specific factors, it is reasonable to expect that a party could still see electoral benefits to being the incumbent *party* even if an incumbent legislator would not.

The outcome variable for both RDD approaches is the Democratic share of the two-party vote. Erikson and Titiunik's RDD model includes the same incumbency variables as the Gelman and King (1990) estimator, but also includes the lagged congressional vote, district-level presidential vote, and year fixed effects. As noted earlier, Erikson and Titiunik estimate this model on the subset of legislators who are first-time incumbents and won an open-seat contest in the previous election. In the partisan incumbency RDD model, incumbency is defined as a binary variable denoting whether a Democratic candidate won the previous election or not, and the analysis focuses on districts that were "close" contests in the previous election.[14] The incumbency measure identifies the electoral benefits accrued by the incumbent party after winning a close election during the previous cycle.[15] As before, we exclude elections immediately after the decennial reapportionment. Since this approach requires us to examine either only first-time incumbents who entered office via an open seat or close elections, we do not have enough cases to estimate yearly models. Therefore, we pool elections by decade to ensure enough cases per period and report the results of these two RDD estimators in Figure 5.3.

In Figure 5.3, the black dots and confidence intervals depict the personal incumbency advantage, while the gray bars and corresponding confidence intervals represent the partisan incumbency advantage. Overall, the estimates for both forms of the incumbency advantage follow a similar trend as those evident in earlier figures, which suggests that both

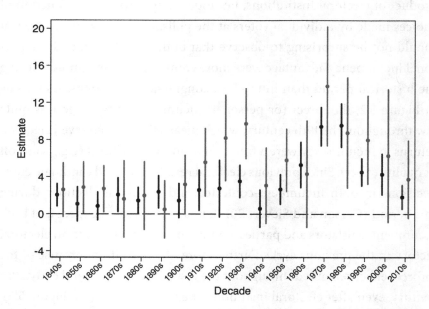

**Figure 5.3** Personal and Partisan Incumbency Advantage RDD Estimates by Decade

estimators pick up on the same basic dynamics reported in previous studies. What is of more immediate interest, however, are the changes in these estimates during periods of low and high nationalization. While the personal and partisan incumbency estimates were of comparable magnitude, 9.2 and 10.7, respectively, during the realigning period (1968–1990), the same cannot be said for the most recent years. The estimate for the partisan incumbency advantage drops to 7.2, but the change is quite modest compared to the personal incumbency advantage, which drops just over 5 percentage points down to 4.1. The sizable decrease in the personal incumbency advantage during the most recent period is consistent with our expectation that the direct benefit of incumbency should be undermined by nationalization. It is important to note, however, that an incumbent *party* is still advantaged electorally during this period of increased nationalization. This also appears to be the case during the late 19th century, albeit to a lesser extent.

These results can also speak to our earlier point about the substantive difference between nationalization today and nationalization during the 19th century. During the 19th century nationalization was largely the product of electoral institutions, but today it appears to be a function of choices made by individual voters at the polls. Given these differences, it should not be surprising to observe that both the partisan and the personal incumbency advantage were more comparable in magnitude during the historical period than in modern congressional elections. As we saw in Figure 5.2, the direct (or personal) incumbency advantage was quite low throughout the 19th century, which means that the observed electoral returns to incumbency were a function of an indirect effect (e.g., scare-off or quality effect). Since previous electoral results informed candidate entry decisions in both incumbent-contested and open-seat elections during this period (Carson and Sievert 2017), it is reasonable to expect that both incumbent legislators and parties would see similar returns to an electoral victory in the previous cycle. Furthermore, the overall importance of the indirect effect remained throughout the rest of the late 19th and early 20th century, even after electoral institutions began to change (see Figure 5.2), which likely accounts for the results during the period from 1890 to 1930.

## Nationalization and the Indirect Effects of Incumbency

While our finding that the different regression-based measures of incumbency follow a comparable trend over time is of note, the overall estimates provide only a partial account of the forces driving the incumbency advantage. Our argument is that nationalization should diminish the personal, or in Cox and Katz's (1996) terms, the direct effect of incumbency more clearly than other components of the incumbency advantage. Indeed, the robust evidence of candidate quality effects and strategic candidate entry during earlier periods of nationalized elections (Carson and Sievert 2017, 2018) suggests that the indirect components—scare-off and quality effects—might be less susceptible to the effects of nationalization. To explore these dynamics, we examine variation in the direct and indirect components of the Cox-Katz measure over time as well as the scare off effect, which are reported in Figure 5.4.

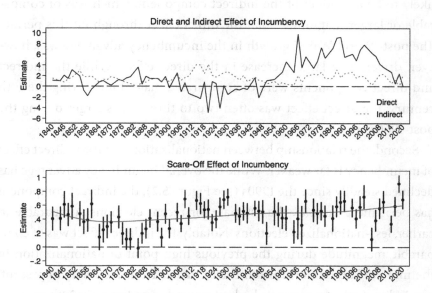

**Figure 5.4** Incumbency Effects from Cox-Katz Estimator by Year
NOTE: The black dots denote the coefficient estimate for the scare-off effect while the black lines report the 95 percent confidence intervals. The gray line is a loess smoother.

In the top panel of Figure 5.4, the black line reports the direct effect of incumbency as derived from the Cox-Katz regression-based estimator. The direct effect of incumbency exhibits a noticeable jump that occurs in the late 1960s and is followed by a downturn in the 1990s that has continued in recent elections. These trends are consistent with Jacobson's (2015b) expectations about the impact of nationalization on the incumbency advantage. Notably, the estimate for the direct effect of incumbency is also small in magnitude and often statistically insignificant during the 19th century, which is consistent with our theoretical expectation that nationalization should, in general, diminish the personal component of incumbency.

The gray dashed line in the top panel of Figure 5.4 reports the indirect effect of incumbency, which is a product of both a candidate quality component and a scare-off effect. These results reveal two interesting patterns. First, the overall incumbency advantage (see Figure 5.2) appears to be driven by different forces across the entire swath of time we examine. During the 19th century, the incumbency advantage was more likely to be a product of the indirect component, which was of comparable or larger magnitude than the direct effect throughout this period. The post–World War II growth in the incumbency advantage was, however, driven by a large increase in the direct effect. While the indirect and direct components were of comparable magnitude during the 19th century, the direct effect was often two to three times larger during the post-1960s era.

Second, the relationship between nationalization and the indirect effect of incumbency is far weaker. While the overall incumbency advantage has declined steadily since the 1990s (see Figure 5.2), the indirect component has been more volatile, the estimate for recent elections comparable to earlier, less-nationalized elections. Notably, the indirect effect was of comparable magnitude during the previous high point of nationalization in the mid- to late 19th century to the estimates from the 1960s to present. The indirect effect reaches its highest point during the early 20th century, a time when both the overall incumbency advantage and the direct effect were quite low. The growth of the indirect effect in these decades is notable since candidate-centered elections began to emerge during this period (Carson and Roberts 2013; Ware 2002).

We also explored the individual components—scare-off and quality effect—of the indirect effect of incumbency. For now, we focus specifically on the scare-off component since, like the direct effect, it is based on a comparison of incumbents and nonincumbents. In the bottom panel of Figure 5.4, we report the coefficient estimate for scare-off along with the corresponding 95 percent confidence intervals. We also applied a loess smoother to the data, depicted by the gray line, to explore any potential trends over time. While the overall (Figure 5.2) and direct (Figure 5.4) effects of incumbency moved in tandem with changes in nationalization, the scare-off effect shows no such relationship. Indeed, the scare-off effect has been comparatively stable since the 1920s and is in fact higher now than during the less nationalized period of the 1940s and 1950s. During the historical era, there once again does not appear to be a clear relationship with nationalization. While the scare-off effect was quite pronounced early in the party ballot era, it drops markedly in the 1860s and 1870s but begins to rebound as electoral reforms like the Australian ballot and direct primary are adopted. In short, while changes in nationalization may impact the direct electoral returns to incumbency, it appears to be largely unrelated to more indirect effects like an incumbent's ability to discourage higher-quality candidates from entering a race.[16]

## NATIONAL FORCES AND ELECTION OUTCOMES

While these initial results are quite informative, we believe it is important to examine the impact of nationalization more closely. We accomplish this in two respects. First, we examine how election timing influenced the incumbency advantage during the party ballot era. We leverage variation in the expected level of nationalization both across and within elections during the 19th century. If nationalization impacts incumbency, we should see the estimated effect change in predictable ways as nationalization increases and decreases. Second, we compare the predictive power of regression analysis that includes only national-level forces, such as partisanship or presidential vote, against a regression model that includes both national and local forces. Since nationalized elections imply that top-down forces, such as presidential vote or partisanship, are the primary factors that shape election outcomes (Hopkins 2018), the second model should add little in the way of explanatory power during periods of high nationalization. When nationalization wanes, however, local forces, like incumbency, should provide additional explanatory power above and beyond national forces.

### Election Timing and Nationalization

It is widely recognized that the party-supplied ballots that were in use for much of the 19th century made it nearly impossible for voters to cast a split-ticket vote (Engstrom and Kernell 2005; Rusk 1970). Although the rate of split-ticket voting was far lower in this era, we expect two factors to condition the nationalization of congressional elections and thereby enhance the role of incumbency. First, the non-uniform election dates for congressional elections meant that there was meaningful variation in the association between congressional and presidential elections or broader national trends (Engstrom and Kernell 2005). Second, the absence of the president from the midterm ballot should weaken the nationalization of elections and increase the importance of incumbency.

In Table 5.1, we report a series of estimates examining the influence of nationalized elections on the incumbency advantage from 1840 to 1870.[17] The first set of estimates are for both midterm and presidential elections. As expected, the incumbency advantage is higher in midterm elections than in presidential elections, 2.7 and 1.6 percentage points, respectively. More interesting, however, the Cox-Katz measures suggest that the difference is driven entirely by the direct component. The estimated direct effect in midterm elections is 1.2 percentage points, but approximately 0.6 percentage points in presidential elections. In contrast, the difference

Table 5.1 INCUMBENCY ADVANTAGE ESTIMATES BY ELECTION TYPE, 1840–1870

|  | Gelman-King | Cox-Katz Direct | Indirect | Overall |
|---|---|---|---|---|
| Midterm | 2.70 (1.73, 3.69) | 1.24 | 2.00 | 3.24 |
| Presidential | 1.64 (0.75, 2.52) | 0.58 | 1.77 | 2.35 |
| Non-November | 1.78 (0.72, 2.84) | 0.78 | 1.36 | 2.29 |
| November | 1.39 (−0.06, 2.84) | 0.07 | 1.51 | 1.59 |

NOTE: Cell entries are estimates of the incumbency advantage based on Equation 5.1 (Gelman-King) and Equations 5.2 and 5.3 (Cox-Katz). 95% confidence intervals presented in parentheses.

between midterm and presidential elections (in terms of the estimated indirect effect) is minimal, 2 and 1.8 percentage points, respectively.

One advantage of turning to historical elections is that the nonuniform election timing allows us to exploit the variation in nationalization *within* the same election year. The uniformity of contemporary congressional elections means that Jacobson's (2015b) analysis was limited to a comparison of data over time because there is no cross-sectional variation. As such, the variation in electoral rules during the 19th century provides a unique opportunity to test Jacobson's theoretical argument. Specifically, we estimated the Gelman-King and Cox-Katz models separately for elections held in November and those held outside of November. We report the results of this analysis in the final three rows of Table 5.1.

As Jacobson (2015b) suggests, the incumbency advantage is approximately twice as large in congressional elections held after the November presidential election for both measures. We once again see that the increased effect is derived almost entirely from an increase in the direct effect of incumbency. For congressional elections held in November of a presidential election year, the direct effect is approximately 0, but was over 1.3 percentage points for elections held outside of November. In contrast, the indirect effect in November elections, 1.5 percentage points, was more comparable to the estimates for non-November elections, approximately 1.4 percentage points. In sum, we not only find differences in the size of the incumbency advantage across election years, but we also find interesting variation in the incumbency advantage within a single election year. As the relative influence of national and local forces changed, the incumbency advantage moved in response. Indeed, the benefits of incumbency were clearly important at times when elections were more likely to be influenced by local, rather than national, considerations.

## National and Local Predictors of Election Outcomes

The outcome variable for this analysis is coded 1 if a Democrat won and 0 if a Whig or Republican won. Since our outcome variable is binary, we use logistic regression models for our analysis. In the first regression model, the only predictor is the district-level Democratic presidential vote, which captures national-level forces. For the second regression model, we include both presidential vote and the measure of incumbency discussed. We then calculate the proportion of cases correctly predicted (PCP) for both sets of models. The PCP for Model 1 provides an indication of how well a national-forces-only model explains election outcomes. As indicated above, under a highly nationalized electoral environment, this single covariate should correctly predict the partisan outcome of a high percentage of House elections. To ascertain whether incumbency adds additional explanatory power, we take the difference between the PCP for Models 1 and 2. As this second quantity approaches zero, we can infer that incumbency adds little explanatory power, which would be consistent with partisan-centered, nationalized elections. When the difference between the PCP for these two models increases, we can infer that incumbency helps to capture important differences between districts that are otherwise similar with respect to their presidential vote share.

For the first step of our analysis, we estimated the model outlined above by decade for all districts as well as marginal districts.[18] The comparison across district types is important because nationalization should have the same effect regardless of district-level competitiveness. Since the number of cases in a given year for marginal districts can be relatively small, we pooled the data by decade to ensure there was an adequate number of cases and to allow for a comparison over time. The first panel in Figure 5.5 reports the findings for all districts, while the second panel reports the estimates for marginal districts.

As expected, the regression model with only presidential vote (Model 1) correctly predicts a large share of election outcomes for the pooled model during the party ballot era (between 75 and 85 percent) and the prior two decades (84 and 92 percent, respectively), both periods of high nationalization. Similarly, the addition of incumbency (Model 2) offers only slight improvements to our predictive power in either period. From the 1840s to the 1890s, for instance, the difference in PCP between Model 1 and Model 2 approaches zero. During the most recent decade, the inclusion of incumbency adds a modest 2.5 percentage points to our predictive power and a more sizable 8.3 percentage points for the early 2000s. It is important to note that although the predictive power of the

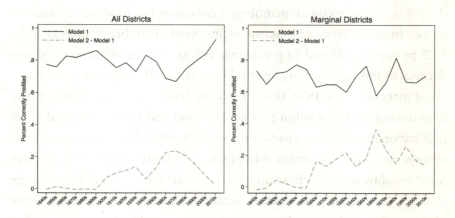

**Figure 5.5** Comparison of Model Predictions, All Cases and Marginal Districts
NOTE: The solid black line denotes the PCP for Model 1, while the dashed gray line denotes the difference between the PCP for Model 2 and Model 1.

presidential vote is the same across the two periods, the inclusion of incumbency, at least in the early 2000s, did produce a modest improvement in our explanatory power. These differences are consistent with our prior observation that while the consequences of nationalization may be the same across the two periods, the mechanisms underlying this process—one institutional and the other voter choices—will differ. Indeed, the removal of the institutional barriers to voter choice means that while *most* voters choose to cast a straight ticket today, incumbency does help us explain the outcome of at least a nontrivial number of cases. It is, of course, important to note that this 8-percentage-point increase is far smaller than the 15- or 20-percentage-point increase during the less nationalized mid-20th century.

Although the findings for the pooled model comport with expectations of prior research on nationalization, the analysis of marginal districts tells a different story. As before, presidential vote alone explains a high percentage, usually around 70 percent, of election outcomes during the party ballot era. Similarly, the inclusion of incumbency does little to improve the model's explanatory power during this era, between 0 and 4 percentage points. We find a different pattern, however, during the modern era. While presidential vote still predicts the outcome in most marginal races, between 65 and 70 percent in each decade since the 1970s except for the 1980s, the inclusion of incumbency continues to add some explanatory power. In the 1970s and 1990s, the inclusion of incumbency increased the PCP by between 23 and 25 percentage points. For the 1980s and first two decades of the 20th century, we find between an 11- and a 16-percentage-point increase in the PCP. While there are fewer marginal districts today than during the party ballot period (Jacobson and Carson 2020), the fact that nationalization is a product of voter choice rather than institutional arrangements has important consequences in these competitive districts. Most notably, while partisanship and national forces still explain a large share of the variance in election outcomes, incumbency explains some of this variance above and beyond what was possible during a period of institution-induced nationalization.

Nationalization and Incumbency

For the second stage of our analysis, we conduct an analysis similar to the one reported in Figure 5.5 but focus on comparisons in presidential and midterm elections. During the party ballot period, nationalization varied across presidential and midterm years (Carson and Sievert 2017).[19] In the modern era, nationalization does not ebb and flow based on whether the president is on the ballot (Jacobson 2019a). We therefore should expect to find differences across election types for the two periods of nationalized elections. While the district-level presidential vote should explain a high percentage of election outcomes in the party ballot era, it should be less predictive of midterm election outcomes. When nationalization is a product of voter choice rather than institutions, however, there should be little difference between presidential and midterm elections.

In Figure 5.6, we report the PCP for Model 1 for presidential election years (black line) and the PCP for Model 1 for midterm years (gray dashed line). During the party ballot era, district-level presidential vote explains

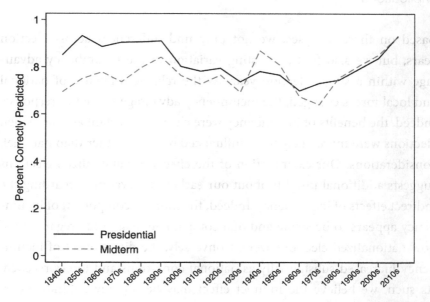

**Figure 5.6** Comparison of Model Predictions, Presidential and Midterm Election Years
NOTE: The solid black line denotes the PCP for Model 1 during presidential election years, and the dashed gray line denotes the PCP for Model 1 during midterm election years.

between 85 and 90 percent of election outcomes. These figures are roughly comparable to the prior two decades and between 10 and 20 percentage points higher than any decade during the 20th century. There are differences, however, between the two periods when we examine midterm elections. While presidential vote predicts a comparable share of congressional midterm election outcomes during the 20th century, it has far less explanatory power during the party ballot period. Across the five decades in which the party ballot was in use, presidential vote alone never explains more than 79 percent of election outcomes—which occurs during the 1880s—and is as low as 69 percent in the 1840s. As such, the PCP for midterm years is frequently 15 to 20 percentage points lower between presidential and midterm election years, which is consistent with prior findings about how ballot laws influenced nationalization during the 19th century.

## Implications

Based on these analyses, we not only find differences across election years, but we also find interesting variation in the incumbency advantage within a single election year. As the relative influence of national and local forces changed, the incumbency advantage moved in response. Indeed, the benefits of incumbency were clearly important at times when elections were more likely to be influenced by local, rather than national, considerations. Our examination of the effects of nationalized elections suggests additional insights about our earlier observations regarding the indirect effects of incumbency. Indeed, the indirect component of incumbency appears to be stable and of a comparable magnitude regardless of how nationalized elections were. Conversely, the direct effect of incumbency increased substantially as national conditions and forces receded. As such, we believe the indirect effect may be the key behind understanding the incumbency advantage throughout many of the historical elections included in our analysis. Nevertheless, the direct benefits of incumbency were equally as important when elections were more likely to be influenced by local, rather than national, considerations.

## SUMMARY

Despite the enormous attention given to the incumbency advantage in the congressional elections literature, there are still several unanswered questions about its underlying causes, explanations for the variation in the benefits of being an incumbent, and its direct implications for democratic governance. Based on our analysis of the incumbency advantage over a longer time span than in previous analyses, several conclusions are clear. First, incumbents have nearly always been advantaged by their position in office, and the size of that advantage has fluctuated over time with changing political conditions, such as levels of nationalization. As such, the recent decline in the incumbency advantage (Jacobson 2015b) is a return to a more typical historical pattern.

More important from the perspective of democratic theory, institutional features can cause fluctuations in the overall effect of incumbency on electoral outcomes, but this advantage persists across a large variety of institutional designs and norms. It may well be that an electoral system based on single-member districts will always afford some advantage to the incumbent, which will in turn depress competition. Future research should therefore focus on other factors—both institutional and extrainstitutional—that are constant in some way across time and help to establish a baseline of support for incumbent House candidates.

Second, the increased incumbency advantage during the latter half of the 20th century was likely anomalous and a product of markedly lower levels of nationalization.[20] It is important to note that we do find some evidence, however, of a direct incumbency advantage across earlier historical periods. Our results suggest the magnitude of the incumbency advantage was a function of the nationalization of elections and the electoral rules and institutions in place at the time. In this way, our results comport with prior studies that find evidence of variation in the incumbency advantage due to various electoral reforms, including adoption of the Australian ballot, the demise of patronage, adoption of primary elections, and further balloting and technological changes in the 20th century (Carson and Roberts 2013).

More recent changes to the levels of nationalization seen in elections could be attributed to a variety of factors. Our findings, particularly the comparative stability of the scare-off effect, comport with other work that focuses on the supply of candidates (Thomsen 2017). A decrease in the supply of moderate candidates who run for Congress would no doubt lead to a decrease in split-ticket voting as voters are primarily presented with two polarized options. In future research, it could be informative to engage in a more direct test (e.g., survey experiments) of the connection between the supply of candidates and the nationalization of elections. Another explanation for more recent nationalization is the collapse of regional differences within parties. Indeed, there are now fewer regional differences in the types of candidates elected to represent each party (McCarty, Poole, and Rosenthal 2016), and the connection between presidential and subpresidential elections varies less by region than it did only a few decades ago (Sievert and McKee 2019).[21]

Third, there is considerable disagreement in the literature over the causes and growth of the incumbency advantage. Much of that disagreement stems from an examination of roughly the same 50- to 60-year period during the modern era. In fact, there is even a dispute over whether the advantages accruing to incumbents are more partisan or personal (Erikson 2016). By extending our analysis of the incumbency advantage across time and employing several different measures, we find that the era given the most attention (from the 1960s onward) is an outlier when compared with the much wider period of history in our analysis. Therefore, our understanding of the incumbency advantage may be biased by the fact that nearly all studies have observed this effect at its peak.

Additional work on the effects of incumbent status on electoral outcomes will need to consider the broader trends of this phenomenon as discussed in this chapter. It is important for future research to also focus on the substantive implications of this work. Why are incumbents so advantaged, and what does this imply for the health of democracy in this nation? What role do voters play in the incumbency advantage? Are they simply too indifferent to and disengaged from politics to concern themselves with holding incumbents accountable, except for extreme cases? If so, what can be done—if anything—to combat this? Similarly, does this effect carry over to other offices, both state and federal, in magnitude and across time? It would follow that increased nationalization does not stop with federal offices, and we expect that uncovering the relationship between incumbency and other elected positions would further bolster the findings we have presented here.

# 6

# Nationalization and Polarization

For at least the past two decades, pundits and scholars alike have debated the origins, consequences of, and possible remedies for the increasing partisan polarization in the United States. As McCarty, Poole, and Rosenthal (2016) demonstrate, the country is now more polarized than at any other period in our nation's history. Although these authors place much of the blame for polarization on the growth of income inequality and replacement among members of Congress, the extant literature offers no shortage of competing explanations. Theriault (2008), for instance, argues that rank-and-file members have ceded more power to party leaders over time, which has allowed leaders to exert greater control over the procedures that govern the legislative process. The result has been an increase in polarization that is driven by what makes it to the floor for a vote in Congress. In contrast, other scholars contend that changes in the supply of moderate candidates, which stem from more polarized voters participating in congressional primaries, account for much of the increase in polarization (Hall 2019; Theriault 2006; Thomsen 2014, 2017).

Bonica and Cox (2018) offer yet another account for the rather dramatic increase in polarization in the contemporary Congress. They accept the contention that ideological replacement has contributed to some of the polarization in Congress, but also argue that increased partisan competition for control of the U.S. House has spurred ideological migration that accounts for as much as 40 percent of recent partisan polarization. Bonica and Cox point to partisan donors who contribute a greater share of money in individual races as a key factor that makes it more difficult for representatives to escape blame for their parties' actions and behavior. In short, individual legislators have become more firmly attached to the party brand, with potentially disastrous consequences when the electorate perceives one of the two major parties negatively. According to Bonica and Cox, this pattern has become especially pronounced since 1994 and has led to increased levels of polarization during the past two decades.

In this chapter, we seek to assess the validity of these competing explanations for partisan polarization in the U.S. Congress. Unlike much of the existing research, however, we argue that we cannot hope to fully adjudicate the competing claims by looking at levels of polarization only in the modern era. Instead, we investigate patterns of partisan polarization across a much larger swath of history. Specifically, our account focuses on the interactive effects of the declining levels of competition in Congress, the replacement of members in both new and open seats, and the dramatic changes in the nationalization of elections over time. It is this last factor especially that helps us more systematically understand why we have witnessed fluctuations in polarization and what potential steps may be taken to try to reduce it in the future.

As this chapter shows, there is a strong relationship between nationalization and polarization regardless of the political era. Before we discuss this more systematically, it is useful to contextualize this phenomenon with a recent example. Our theoretical argument is illustrated quite clearly by the career of Eric Cantor, a lawyer and former Republican member who represented the 7th district of Virginia in the U.S. House of Representatives. Cantor was first elected to the House in 2000 after representing the 73rd district in the Virginia House of Delegates since 1992. Cantor was elected as the House minority whip in 2009 thanks to his strong party loyalty and conservative credentials and served until 2011, when he became the House majority leader. He was viewed by many as the natural successor to Speaker John Boehner because of his position and favorable reputation among many of the party faithful.

Cantor's political future changed dramatically in 2014 when his promising career trajectory was cut short due to a surprising primary defeat.

During Cantor's time in the leadership, members of the "Tea Party" faction within the Republican caucus felt that he was becoming too moderate on several issues, especially immigration. Cantor also spent very little time in his Virginia district and was perceived by a growing segment of his constituents as out of touch with their views. In the 2014 Republican primary, Cantor's challenger was a little-known college professor from Randolph-Macon College, David Brat, who received strong backing from the Tea Party during the primary. Although Cantor had a 10:1 spending advantage over Brat in the primary, Brat ultimately prevailed, winning 55.5 percent of the vote compared to Cantor's 44.5 percent.

Cantor's primary loss sent shockwaves throughout the Republican Party and was labeled by many media outlets as one of the most shocking primary election results in the modern era.[1] His defeat also represented the first time a sitting House majority leader had lost a primary election. Although the media and pundits mentioned a variety of factors contributing to his electoral defeat, the highly nationalized political environment and the growing discord within the ranks of the Republican caucus were among the most salient in this surprising upset. Cantor had a conservative voting record, but the voters who turned out to support Brat believed he was not conservative *enough* on the issues that ultimately mattered to them.

## CONGRESSIONAL POLARIZATION ACROSS TIME

Congressional scholars often view the 1970s as the starting point of increased ideological polarization between the Democratic and Republican parties (see, e.g., Abramowitz, Alexander, and Gunning 2006; Ladewig 2010; Poole and Rosenthal 1984; Theriault 2006, 2008). The 1970s also witnessed a notable decline in the number of competitive seats. Although one might expect these two trends to be causally related, it is important to recall that the national parties were similarly polarized in the late 1800s and early 1900s (Poole and Rosenthal 2007), during which time there was significantly more electoral competition (Carson and Roberts 2013).

Another notable difference between the two periods is that congressional candidates today are selected in a more democratic fashion than during the late 19th century (Ware 2002). Even though party organizations now have less control over candidate nominations, contemporary candidates and legislators still tend to be more ideologically consistent with the rest of their party (Thomsen 2014).

As noted above, there is no shortage of potential explanations in existing works for the increased polarization in Congress since the 1970s. Theriault (2006, 2008), for instance, attributes much of the growth in polarization to two critical factors that have occurred during the past 40 years: the ideological and partisan alignment of each party's constituencies and the decision by rank-and-file members to cede greater amounts of authority to their party leaders. The second factor is especially important since it allows floor leaders to utilize procedural tools to achieve more favorable partisan outcomes by keeping certain bills off the floor while allowing others to come to a vote in Congress. Theriault concludes that most of the rise in polarization in the House can be attributed to the increasing frequency of these procedural tools in the context of the legislative process.[2]

Another popular explanation for increased polarization, especially in the media, is that primary elections have contributed to the extreme divisiveness observed in the modern Congress. The argument is that as the number of extreme voters participating in primary elections increases, it leads to ideologically extreme candidates getting selected to run in the general election. Over time, more ideologically extreme members replace the moderate candidates who formerly ran and were elected, which results in greater levels of polarization on both sides of the aisle. More recently, several studies have advanced a version of this argument by suggesting that congressional polarization is driven by an increasing supply of ideologically motivated candidates (Hall 2019; Thomsen 2014, 2017). Thomsen (2014) finds moderates are less likely to believe they can win the primary and therefore are less likely to run for, or see value in, a House seat. These dynamics result in general election voters being presented with a choice between two candidates who are more polarized than would be expected based on voter preferences.

McCarty, Poole, and Rosenthal (2009, 2016) have made valuable contributions to our understanding of the shifting patterns of polarization over time. First, McCarty, Poole, and Rosenthal (2009) responded to the increased emphasis on gerrymandering as a potential source of polarization. While both popular and scholarly accounts suggest that decreases in electoral competition caused by redistricting led to greater levels of polarization, their results indicate that "congressional polarization is primarily a function of the differences in how Democrats and Republicans represent the same districts rather than a function of which districts each party represents or the distribution of constituency preferences" (666). Based on a series of simulations to evaluate the level of polarization under a variety of "neutral" districting practices, McCarty, Poole, and Rosenthal find little difference between the observed levels of polarization and those produced via their simulations.

Second, McCarty, Poole, and Rosenthal (2016) offer one of the most systematic studies on the potential factors that have contributed to polarization since the late 19th and early 20th centuries. While acknowledging that the United States is now more polarized than at any other point in history, they also reject a number of the existing explanations for polarization that focus primarily on the modern era. In placing much of the blame for increased levels of polarization on the growth of income inequality, demographic trends, and member replacement, they dismiss procedural arguments or explanations rooted in practices such as gerrymandering as the driving source for polarization in Congress.

The aforementioned discussion points to an important consideration when scholars discuss the potential causes of congressional polarization. Namely, we need to be attentive to whether a potential factor offers explanatory power across different historical eras. In the same way that McCarty, Poole, and Rosenthal (2009, 2016) argue against gerrymandering as the primary source of polarization given that the Senate (where redistricting does not occur) is nearly as polarized as the House, we maintain that the supply of candidates via primary elections cannot be a *time invariant* cause of increased polarization. After all, the ideological divide between the congressional parties was also high during the late 19th century well before the emergence of the direct primary. Our argument is consistent with Hirano et al.'s (2010) research on the history of primary elections, which dismisses their role in contributing directly to polarization in Congress. If anything, the use of primaries may have only enhanced existing levels of polarization that were already in place rather than directly contributing to it.

Although each of the preceding explanations differs with respect to the changing patterns of polarization over time, one thing they tend to have in common is that they focus largely on macro-level factors such as political institutions (i.e., gerrymandering or institutional changes) or income inequality. Our goal is not to dismiss the importance of such explanations out of hand but to instead focus on micro-level explanations to offer a more dynamic perspective on congressional polarization. We do so by using a longer period of elections to better understand the interactive effects of the declining levels of candidate competition over time, replacement of legislators in both new and open seats, as well as fundamental changes in the degree to which elections have become more or less nationalized. We believe that nationalized elections will produce ideologically extreme candidates who respond to national party interests rather than local district conditions, as was common through the mid-20th century (Jacobson and Carson 2020).

Our argument about competition and nationalization is consistent with work by Merrill, Grofman, and Brunell (2014), who explore the relationship between the national party and constituency-based electoral considerations in partisan polarization. Their formal model of electoral competition emphasizes the role of national party constraints on a candidate's ability to locate themselves at an ideological position that is dissimilar from the national party. In their own words, they maintain:

> In relatively liberal districts "moderately liberal" candidates of the more conservative party may be defeated, since they will be unable to present themselves credibly as liberals. Similarly, in relatively conservative districts "moderately conservative" candidates of the more liberal party are disadvantaged, since their conservative credentials

will be questioned (cf. Grofman et al., 2000). Only when there is strong regional differentiation of the parties . . . can candidates out of tune with the national party position present fully credible claims to track the median voter in their district. Absent such special conditions, the more strongly are the parties differentiated at the national level, the harder it will be for a candidate of a party whose national position is located far from the district median to win. (Merrill, Grofman, and Brunell 2014, 551)

Indeed, their observation is consistent with research on the ideological positioning of congressional candidates. Based on an examination of the ideological positions of candidates in elections from the post-Reconstruction period to the mid-1990s, Ansolabehere, Snyder, and Stewart (2001) find that in certain historical periods, candidates were more responsive to the ideological positions of the national parties than to their constituents. The late 19th and early 20th century and the period from the 1980s onward were both marked by candidates who "primarily espoused the ideology associated with the national party, moderating very little to accommodate local ideological conditions" (136). Bafumi and Herron (2010) reach a similar conclusion after analyzing member replacement in the 109th (2005–2006) and 110th (2007–2008) Congresses. They contend that cross-party replacements lead to "leapfrog representation, the phenomenon that occurs when one extremist in the House or Senate is replaced by another extremist" (538). These dramatic changes in legislator ideology are the result of new representatives being more responsive to the national party than to the district median.

While there are clear normative implications for the existence of leapfrog representation, it is important to note that it does not necessarily indicate that voters are always dissatisfied with or overly punitive toward these new legislators. Indeed, Jacobson (2000) notes that polarization depends, at least in part, on the expectation that voters would reward, or at least not punish, legislators who voted the party line. Jacobson's observation is particularly important considering the recent increase in partisan loyalty in congressional elections (Jacobson and Carson 2020). When considered together, each of the previous studies gives us reason to believe the nationalization of elections could be an important force underlying fluctuations in polarization—an idea we will explore further in the remainder of the chapter.

## ELECTORAL COMPETITION AND POLARIZATION

Competitive elections are an integral component of a democratic system that periodically allows citizens to voice their opinions (Dahl 1971). Indeed, elections are an important, albeit blunt, instrument with which voters exert influence and control over their elected officials. Competition, however, is necessarily linked to the array of choices available to voters. As Krasno (1994, 5) observed, electoral competition requires that voters are "faced with viable options and make their choices. But if the deck is somehow stacked so that one candidate is virtually guaranteed victory, then public accountability is undermined." Although a considerable amount of attention has been given to the decline in electoral competition in recent decades, congressional elections have varied in their degree of competitiveness over time (Carson and Roberts 2013).

Mayhew's (1974a) examination of the "vanishing marginals" provides a useful starting point in comparing influences on competition in House elections. Mayhew notes that over time, fewer members of the House came from "competitive" districts, those where the incumbent won with less than 60 percent of the vote. Additionally, he found that legislators were, on average, winning by larger margins than had been the case in the past. Jacobson (1987) challenges this claim—specifically the idea that the marginals were stable over time. Instead, he finds that members from safe districts became more likely to lose in a subsequent election due to the increased volatility in the interelection vote swing.

Jacobson's work led scholars to debate the proper measurement of electoral marginality (see, e.g., Bauer and Hibbing 1989; Jacobson 1993). Jacobson (1987, 128) made a particularly important contribution to this debate in noting that winning or losing matters most and that "the size of the victory or loss is of decidedly secondary importance." Wilkins (2012) builds on this observation in his examination of the probability that from 1900 to 2006 a House incumbent was or would have been defeated. He finds a steady decline in the probability of an incumbent defeat until around 1950, at which point it settles into a new mean level. Wilkins's findings provide support for Jacobson's earlier observation that incumbents were no more likely to win in the 1950s than they were in the 1980s. One important insight, though, is that the mean level of security Jacobson observed differs meaningfully from the average level of incumbent electoral security in the first half of the 20th century.[3]

Despite the extensive literature on declining electoral competition, not everyone agrees with this conclusion. As mentioned earlier, Bonica and Cox (2018) contend that greater competition for control of the House majority has led to considerable ideological migration, which has further exacerbated levels of polarization in Congress (see also Lee 2016). Increased attention to majority status in Congress has led activists, donors, and even voters to support candidates who are potentially incongruous ideologically if it furthers the party's collective goal. The result is the election of candidates who are more extreme than may otherwise be expected. Bonica and Cox find that congressional elections have become more party-centered over time, but without a corresponding increase in electoral retribution from the voters. The result has been a greater emphasis on national party image at the expense of local interests.

Although Bonica and Cox's argument raises important questions about the relationship between competition and polarization, we have historical reasons to be skeptical of it. First, electoral competition at the district level, which better captures where candidate competition and entry decisions will occur, has been in steady decline across time. Whether we focus on marginality or electoral security, it is quite clear that modern House elections are largely uncompetitive. As shown in Figure 6.1, the number of competitive elections for U.S. House seats has declined steadily, especially since the 1930s, with a general downward trend since the late 19th century. Between 1872 and 1898, approximately 40 percent of elections

Nationalization and Polarization

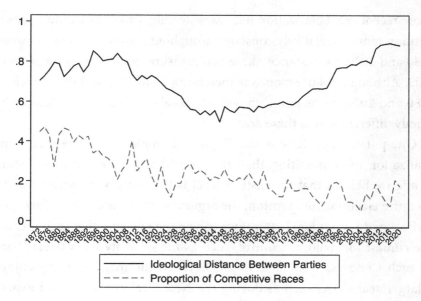

**Figure 6.1** Competitive Races and Polarization, 1872–2020

were decided by 10 percentage points or less. From 1900 to 1944, the last Congress before the postwar era, almost a quarter of races were still competitive. Since that time, though, electoral competition has continued to decline, which has led to the scholarly debate discussed above. Recent congressional elections have been among the least competitive. Since the Republican takeover in 1994, only about 13 percent of races have been competitive, with a remarkably low 5 percent of such races in the 2004 midterms.

Figure 6.1 also plots the relationship between polarization and the competitiveness of House elections from 1872 until 2020. While polarization in Congress was increasing during the latter part of the 19th century, electoral competition in House elections was beginning its downward march. If we limit our focus to the period from 1872 to 1906, which corresponds to a highly party-centered period, the relationship between polarization and competition is quite strong as the two are correlated at −0.77. This changes drastically as competition and ideological distance correlates at 0.25 between 1906 and 1948. We see a very different picture still in the more recent era. Polarization increases steadily, while district-level competition remains relatively constant throughout the modern era. Between 1980 and 2020, for instance, these two measures are correlated at a mere 0.05. Although polarization was increasing from 1872 to 1906 as well as 1980 and 2020, its relationship with electoral competitiveness looks distinctly different across these eras.

One potential critique is that Figure 6.1 employs a different conceptualization of competition than that considered in recent scholarship. While we believe that the district level is the more appropriate way to measure electoral competition, the argument that competition fuels polarization does not fare better if we consider a measure that accounts for the contest for majority control, such as the majority party's seat share in each Congress from 1872 to 2020. When the majority party enjoys a larger seat share, such as during the New Deal era, we would expect competition for control of the House to be lower, on average. Conversely, when majorities are smaller, it is more likely that the next election could produce a change in partisan control. In Figure 6.2 we report the

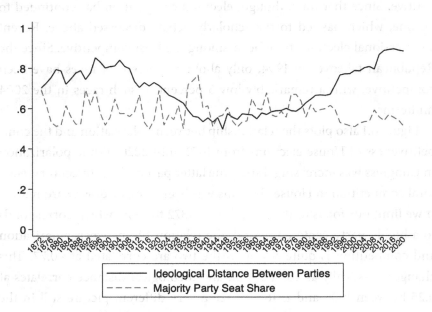

**Figure 6.2** Majority Party Seat Share and Polarization, 1872–2020

majority party's seat share from 1872 to 2020. During the late 19th century, the average majority party seat share was just over 58 percent, but there was also considerable variation in majority size. With some notable exceptions, this general pattern continued throughout much of the 20th century until the 1980s. The real turning point, of course, was the 1994 election, when the Republicans retook control of the House for the first time in four decades. Since that election, the majority party's seat share has averaged around 54 percent.

The differences between the 19th century and the post–Republican Revolution Congresses are important because they further reinforce the limitations of electoral competition as a major driver of polarization. Both periods have been marked by historic levels of polarization, but only the latter has experienced the type of prolonged and heightened competition for majority control that is hypothesized to drive modern congressional partisan conflict. While there is a reasonable negative correlation, −0.57, between polarization and partisan competition since the 1980s, no such trend is present in the 19th century. Taken together, Figures 6.1 and 6.2 indicate that when we examine nearly 150 years of elections rather than only the past few decades, the connection between electoral competition and polarization is far more tenuous. Indeed, *district*-level competition has remained in steady decline, while polarization fluctuates considerably. When we examine competition for control of the House, we find the mirror opposite, where competition is more variable and does not show a clear trend when compared to polarization. In short, arguments centering on electoral competition as driving congressional polarization could simply be an artifact of how competition is operationalized. As such, this leads us to seek an alternative explanation for the fluctuations in polarization over time.

## NATIONALIZED POLITICS AND POLARIZATION

As we documented in Chapter 5, national forces rather than local factors increasingly determine the outcome of House elections. Both greater party loyalty in the electorate and a stronger correlation between presidential and congressional vote shares at the district level point to the increasing nationalization of House elections (Abramowitz and Webster 2016; Davis and Mason 2016; Jacobson 2015a, 2015c; Jacobson and Carson 2020). Based on an analysis of the post–World War II era, Jacobson (2015c, 861) concludes that "Democrats had been the main beneficiaries of the denationalization of electoral politics," but the increased nationalization has advantaged the Republicans and allowed them to win new seats and retain old ones.[4] Coupled with work by Bonica (2014) and McCarty, Poole, and Rosenthal (2016), which shows that Republicans are asymmetrically contributing to greater levels of polarization, it becomes clear that nationalized elections could contribute to greater levels of polarization.

Additionally, the partisan makeup of congressional districts has become significantly more homogeneous over time. As Abramowitz, Alexander, and Gunning (2006, 87) note, "districts held by Democrats are now more strongly Democratic than in the past and districts held by Republicans are now more strongly Republican than in the past." District partisanship is therefore an increasingly important determinant of electoral outcomes and competition (see Chapter 5). There is historical precedent, however, for the patterns uncovered in studies of contemporary House elections. Jenkins, Schickler, and Carson (2004), for instance, found evidence of increased polarization between and homogeneity within Democratic and Republican districts throughout the late 19th century. Indeed, these district-level changes correspond quite well with the rise in polarization that began in the post-Reconstruction era and continued through the early part of the 20th century.

In conjunction with this research, it makes intuitive sense that nationalization and polarization would move in tandem with one another. In periods when nationalization is low, a moderate candidate may be able to attract support from voters of the opposite party to win a seat in Congress. As nationalization increases, however, ideological congruity may fail to lead a candidate to victory if he or she affiliates with the "wrong" party.

This leads us to believe that if primaries are producing more ideologically extreme candidates, as some of the previous literature suggests, then nationalization likely provides the mechanism by which these candidates actually become members of Congress.

Similarly, during the 19th century, the party ballot and party nominating convention provided mechanisms by which more extreme candidates could win seats in Congress. Regardless of ideological placement, a House candidate had a much greater chance of obtaining office if he was from the same party as the presidential candidate who won his district. Even in races that did not occur at the same time as the presidential election, as we show in Chapter 5, it was in the interest of party leaders to nationalize elections as much as possible—or at least capitalize on them—to unseat incumbents who were a better ideological fit with the district but who identified with the less popular party. As Jacobson (2015b, 86) succinctly states, increased nationalization means "House incumbents . . . have a much harder time retaining districts that lean toward the rival party."

As we have demonstrated, scholars have identified a wide variety of methods by which polarization has increased over time. However, many of them do not fully explain this trend outside of the modern era. One that does is suggested by McCarty, Poole, and Rosenthal (2016), in which they attribute rising income inequality to the growth of polarization over time. Related to this, Jacobson (2015b, 861) argues that there have been "widening and increasingly coherent partisan divisions in the American electorate" especially since the mid-20th century. Taken together, these studies suggest that as the middle class shrinks, voters begin to see greater differences between the two major political parties. Those with lower incomes are drawn to politicians who favor more redistributive policies, and those with higher levels of income are more likely to support politicians who promise greater tax benefits. Therefore, ideological placement of candidates becomes secondary—or altogether irrelevant—to party platforms. Building on this idea, we suspect that while income inequality may drive congressional polarization, its effect is at least somewhat dependent upon nationalization in elections.

## Nationalization and Polarization across Time

We begin our examination of the relationship between nationalized elections and polarization by comparing whether they move together over time. We use the proportion of split congressional districts—defined as districts where the winning candidates in the congressional and presidential elections are from different parties—to quantify the extent of nationalization. Although there are several potential descriptive measures we could employ, such as the correlation between the presidential and congressional district-level vote, we believe this split-districts measure captures the main underlying theoretical mechanism at work. Many scholars posit that nationalization is a function of more party-centered elections (Bonica and Cox 2018; Jacobson 2015c; Engstrom and Kernell 2005, 2014). The proportion of split districts is both theoretically and empirically appropriate since it captures the overall level of partisan congruence between national (presidential) and local (congressional) election outcomes.

In Figure 6.3, we report the year-to-year changes in polarization (black) and the proportion of split districts (gray) along with loess regression lines to help identify the over-time patterns in each series. Although the changes in both polarization and the proportion of split congressional districts during the post-1970s period are well documented, it is still worth noting that the two series track each other well. From 1980 to 2020, the correlation between polarization and the proportion of split districts is approximately −0.92. In contrast, the correlation between polarization and split districts is only −0.17 during the historical period from 1872 to 1900. The weaker correlation is somewhat misleading, however. During the historical period, the proportion of split districts was far more constant and averaged around 20 percent for elections. From the mid-1970s onward, however, the proportion of split districts has largely been trending downward. The average proportion of split districts was just over 17 percent for elections in the 21st century and dropped to less than 10 percent for elections in 2016, 2018, and 2020.

Nationalization and Polarization

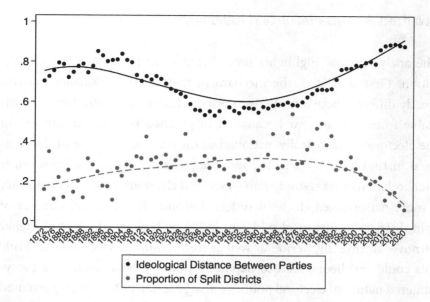

Figure 6.3 Split Congressional Districts and Polarization, 1872–2020

The differences between these two periods, both of which can be fairly classified as eras of nationalized elections, are of note in part because they speak to the different sources of nationalization in each period. Elections during the late 19th and early 20th century were nationalized because the institutions in place at the time, particularly the party ballot, made it nearly impossible to cast a split-ticket vote (Rusk 1970). In short, congressional elections from this era were subject to a form of institutionally induced nationalization. Conversely, the decline of split districts in the modern era is the result of voters choosing to align their votes. Although the result is the same—nationalized elections—it is important to note that the source, institutions versus voters, varies between the two periods. Indeed, we can see this most clearly if we compare midterm and presidential election years during these two periods. During the modern era, the percentage of split districts was 24.3 during presidential years and 31.3 during midterm years. If we focus on just the 21st century, however, the averages are 16.9 and 17.7, respectively, which are substantively identical. From 1872 to 1900, though, the percentage of split districts is 15.8 during presidential years and 25.1 during midterm years.[5]

## Polarized Representation and Nationalized Elections

The analysis above highlights several important points about nationalization. First, as stated, the mechanism that led to nationalization was clearly different between the two periods. Today nationalization remains stable from year to year because of heightened partisan loyalty within the electorate. Historically, nationalization was high because of the electoral institutions in place. The most important implication, however, is that both dynamics result in party-centered elections, which in turn foster a more nationalized electoral system. Second, the increased number of split districts in historical midterm elections is also indicative of higher turnover during this period as well as more competitive elections. While this could, in theory, lead to depolarization, we believe that the party-centered nature of electoral politics during the late 19th century prevented this from happening. Higher turnover and more competitive elections will contribute to polarization if the legislators from opposing parties who replace one another are themselves ideologically extreme. Indeed, Bafumi and Herron (2010) have documented this pattern of "leapfrog representation" in the modern period, but we maintain that it may help us to understand the historical period as well.[6]

As an empirical matter, we believe the key to understanding polarization lies, at least in part, in what happens when Democrats and Republicans represent the "same" district, as alluded to by McCarty, Poole, and Rosenthal (2009). To systematically address this question, we use a legislator's first dimension DW-NOMINATE score as our outcome variable. Our key predictor variables are an indicator for whether the Republican candidate won or not, the district-level Democratic presidential vote (which we treat as a measure of constituent preferences), and the interaction between these two predictors. We also include year and state fixed effects to control for any yearly or subnational factors.[7] Since we have centered the presidential vote measure at 50, the coefficient estimate for the Republican "win" indicator provides an estimate of the difference in DW-NOMINATE scores for a Republican and a Democratic legislator who were elected in a district with a 50-50 split in the presidential vote.

Nationalization and Polarization

The magnitude of this coefficient quantifies the representational difference between the two parties when they win in the "same" district. We expect the partisan gap to be higher when elections are nationalized and lower when local factors are more determinative of the outcome.

Since our interest is how the estimated difference between the two parties changes over time, we estimated the model by decade and report the resulting coefficient estimates in Figure 6.4. We chose to subset the data by decade since it ensured that we had an adequate number of cases in the "close" districts while also allowing us to examine differences across time.[8] The estimated differences in DW-NOMINATE scores between Democrats and Republicans is highest during the 2010s (0.70). These results comport with McCarty, Poole, and Rosenthal's (2016) observation that the House is now the most polarized it has ever been. What is interesting, however, is that although polarization began to rise in the 1970s, it was not until the 1990s that the estimated ideological gap between Republicans and Democrats returned to historic levels. Indeed, the coefficient estimate for the 1990s, 0.63, is comparable to those from the party ballot era of the 1870s and 1880s, which were 0.66 and 0.64, respectively.

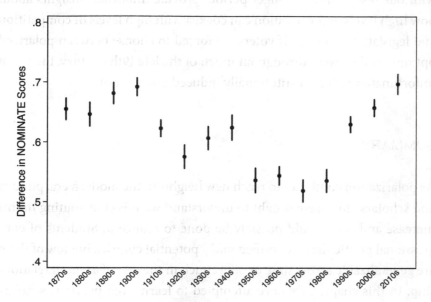

Figure 6.4 Estimated Difference in DW-NOMINATE Scores in Toss-up Districts

Similarly, the results for the 1880s and 1890s—0.68 and 0.69—are higher than in any period from the post–World War II era, aside from the 2010s.

As we noted, the mechanisms that led to more nationalized elections differ across the late 19th century and the contemporary era. What our results show, however, is that regardless of what produces nationalization and the party-centered elections that follow, the result is the same. Indeed, whether nationalization is a result of electoral institutions or voters' partisan loyalty, the supply of legislators becomes increasingly ideological, even in the districts where moderation should—in theory—be electorally advantageous. In this way, our results speak to the overall generalizability of previous studies that focus on the contemporary Congress. First, our results suggest that the leapfrog representation documented by Bafumi and Herron (2010) also took place in the 19th century. Second, our findings support the claim that scholars should be mindful of the candidate, or supply side, of the equation (Ansolabehere, Snyder, and Stewart 2001; Thomsen 2014). As Thomsen (2014, 789) aptly notes, polarization will "persist irrespective of ideological changes in the electorate" if voters are given only polarized options. Indeed, Thomsen's observations, along with our results from a longer period, provide important insights about how high levels of polarization can coexist with high levels of competition and legislative turnover. If voters are forced to choose between polarized options, as they were throughout much of the late 19th century, the result unfortunately will be institutionally induced polarization.

## SUMMARY

As polarization continues to reach new heights in the modern era, pundits and scholars alike have sought to understand what is contributing to this increase and what could possibly be done to reduce it. Students of congressional politics have identified many potential culprits, but few of them are generalizable across time or offer much in the way of a causal relationship. In this chapter, we have attempted to learn from previous scholarship examining the fluctuations in partisan polarization across time. In particular, our findings suggest that the nationalization of elections, regardless of the factors that contributed to the nationalization, provides a means by which the House became more polarized. More specifically, by analyzing split districts in both historical and contemporary eras, we find that high levels of nationalization also correlate with greater levels of polarization. Indeed, we believe that the party-centered nature of elections can help to explain much of the variation in polarization over time.

To be clear, we are not arguing that nationalization of elections is the only factor that is driving the dynamics of polarization across time. Indeed, there appear to be many factors, such as income inequality, primary elections and their effect on candidate emergence, and even electoral competitiveness that can serve to enhance levels of polarization in Congress. Nevertheless, we believe that the degree of election nationalization is a critical explanatory factor that has been previously overlooked when seeking to account for fluctuating levels of polarization across time. As we have shown in the preceding discussion, increased nationalization establishes all the essential components of polarization regardless of what is actually leading to high levels of nationalization. Accordingly, and based on the evidence here, it appears that increased nationalization may be both a necessary and a sufficient condition for higher levels of polarization in Congress.

# 7

# Nationalization and Candidate Evaluations

Leading up to the 2020 election, incumbent president Donald Trump was both historically unpopular and marred by various controversies. As a result, Democrats were eager to remove him from office. Despite an initially poor showing in Iowa and New Hampshire, Joe Biden secured the Democratic nomination after a key victory in South Carolina that led other candidates to drop out and ultimately endorse him. Although he was not especially popular, nor was his candidacy particularly innovative or inspiring, Biden was viewed by many as the best chance for Democrats to win the presidency. Indeed, one poll revealed that a majority of Biden supporters were supporting his candidacy simply because he was not Trump.[1]

Short of winning the presidency, Democratic voters hoped to limit Trump's impact should he win reelection, by electing Democratic majorities in both the U.S. House and U.S. Senate. One manifestation of these ambitions was the emergence of a popular slogan, "Vote Blue No Matter Who." The phrase was used often when discussing politics and elections on social media, and merchandise was sold with the slogan stamped on shirts, hats, and coffee mugs. This trend carried over into the next election cycle with the slogan "Vote Blue in 2022."

The rhetorical strategy to mobilize Democratic voters demonstrates a clear and important trend in the nationalization of recent elections. Voters do not base decisions on individual policy platforms or candidate experience, as had once been the case throughout much of the 20th century when politics was far less nationalized. Voters now gravitate toward one party and advocate for all those party's candidates to win irrespective of who is actually best equipped to represent the needs of an individual state or district. As a result, it has become nearly impossible for a candidate to win in a district or state that leans in the opposite partisan direction in this highly nationalized political environment (Jacobson 2015c; Jacobson and Carson 2020).

While the implications of nationalization for both candidates' electoral prospects and voter decision-making have been explored in recent studies (Abramowitz and Webster 2016; Carson, Sievert, and Williamson 2020; Davis and Mason 2016; Sievert and Banda 2022; Sievert and McKee 2019), we know comparatively less about how the public evaluates congressional candidates in this transformed electoral environment. Understanding how constituents both respond to and assess congressional candidates is important because electoral phenomena like the incumbency advantage and candidate quality depend on voters making distinctions between candidates within the same party (Mann and Wolfigner 1980). If vote choice and candidate evaluations depend solely on partisanship, as the above example implies, then we should observe the public using similar heuristics or cues to evaluate candidates across all House races.

Our primary focus in this chapter is to discern whether the public does in fact see congressional candidates from each party in increasingly uniform terms. We accomplish this through a series of analyses. First, we begin by exploring the determinants of candidate evaluations. Of particular interest is the trend over time in these evaluations and whether there is now greater stability in individual evaluations. Next, we assess the role of presidential politics in the nationalization of candidate evaluations. While extant scholarship has noted the importance of presidents as party leaders, we seek to disentangle president-specific forces from more general partisan evaluations. We conclude with a consideration of how the information environment, in this case local versus national political considerations, impacts candidate evaluations. Throughout these various analyses, we utilize both existing survey data and original survey experimental evidence to better evaluate these specific questions.

## DIMENSIONS OF CANDIDATE EVALUATIONS

Although voters may not always possess detailed knowledge about individual congressional candidates, they can often rely upon certain heuristics to make judgments about a candidate. First, a candidate's partisan affiliation provides important signals about the types of positions she maintains or is likely to hold (Aldrich 2010). Past scholarship has identified several ways that partisanship might inform evaluations of individual candidates. Since parties have established reputations or brands, the public can use this knowledge to make an informed inference about the positions adopted by and issues prioritized by individual candidates (Banda 2016, 2021; Milita et al. 2017; Rahn 1993; Simas 2018). The public may also project their attitudes toward more salient and visible party leaders, such as the president or congressional leadership, onto congressional candidates (Highton 2002; Jacobson 2019b). We would therefore expect that attitudes toward congressional candidates will be tied to how one feels about a given candidate's party and party leaders.

Second, a candidate's connection to or endorsement by certain social and political groups can also be informative signals. This is especially true considering recent increased hostility toward the partisan opposition, which transcends traditional policy disagreements (Mason 2018). The connection between candidates and specific groups can be formed through direct support by the relevant group. For example, interest group endorsements can act as important cues about a candidate's policy positions and priorities (Arceneaux and Kolodny 2009; McDermott 2006). Even in the absence of a group's endorsement, candidates may be linked with particular social groups because the public associates each party with a specific social group (Ahler and Sood 2018; Elder and O'Brian 2022; Miller, Wlezien, and Hildreth 1991). Based on this group-centric understanding of parties, we would expect that knowing a voter's attitudes toward various social groups should help us to predict how she will evaluate candidates from the party associated with those groups.

Third, voters may also evaluate candidates in terms of certain valence characteristics, such as competence or integrity. Early research in this area was particularly interested in understanding whether incumbents enjoyed a character or reputational advantage over their challengers, which might explain at least some of the electoral returns of incumbency (Mann and Wolfinger 1980; Mondak 1995; McCurley and Mondak 1995). Other studies explored how candidate valence influenced candidate strategy (Adams et al. 2011; Stone and Simas 2010) and vote choice (Buttice and Stone 2012). More recent scholarship, however, has added important nuance to our understanding of the role of valence in candidate assessments. Most notably, an individual's partisanship or expressed ideological positions influences her judgment of a candidate's integrity and competence (Simas 2020; Martin 2022). In a more nationalized electoral environment, then, we expect assessment of a congressional candidate's integrity and competence will be driven more by partisanship than by candidate-specific attributes.

Based on these different determinants of candidate evaluations, we identified various survey data that would, where possible, allow us to explore the public's attitudes toward and assessment of congressional candidates over time. While there are instances where data limitations prevent us from exploring these data over a broad period, an examination of these general trends is an important starting point for understanding how nationalization impacts candidate evaluations. As we noted earlier, nationalization should lead voters to hold similar attitudes toward congressional candidates from the same party *regardless* of candidate attributes. We therefore believe it is essential to document these trends first before we move on to assess the underlying mechanism through panel and survey experimental data.

## Partisanship

We begin our analysis of candidate evaluations by analyzing trends in the American National Election Study (ANES). Since the 1980 election, the ANES has asked respondents to rate each major-party House candidate on a thermometer scale. These scales capture one's affect toward a given candidate or group and range from 0 (cold or negative) to 100 (warm or positive), with a score of 50 denoting neutral feelings. In addition to rating each House candidate, respondents were asked about several groups and individuals. These scores allow us to assess, via a correlation coefficient, how attitudes toward congressional candidates relate to assessments of various politically relevant stimuli. For now, we focus on those groups or politicians associated with the parties: the political parties, presidential candidates, and ideological groups. Our primary expectation is that nationalization should yield a tighter correspondence between congressional candidates and these party figures.

In Figure 7.1, we report the correlation between thermometer ratings of congressional candidates and their respective party groups for each presidential election year from 1980 to 2020.[2] Overall, each series follows a similar upward trend across time for both Republican and Democratic House candidates, which is consistent with our expectation that the public

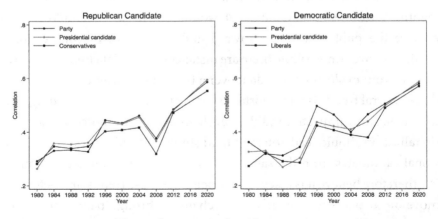

**Figure 7.1** House Candidate and Partisan Feeling Thermometers, 1980–2020

evaluates candidates from the same party in increasingly similar ways. The correlation between evaluations of Republican candidates and their respective party groups follows a nearly identical trend. In 1980, the correlation between thermometer ratings of Republican House candidates and ratings of the Republican Party, Ronald Reagan, and conservatives were 0.29, 0.26, and 0.28, respectively. By the start of the 21st century, the strength of these relationships had steadily increased to a correlation between 0.41 and 0.44. During the 2020 election, the correlation between ratings of the Republican House candidate and ratings of Donald Trump was 0.59, which was more than double the magnitude of the correlation between these same ratings in 1980. The correlation between ratings of Republican congressional candidates and ratings of the Republican Party and conservatives was 0.58 and 0.55, respectively, which is roughly twice as large as the relationships observed 40 years earlier.

The trend for Democratic candidates, while mostly monotonic, is not quite as consistent. For example, the correlation between ratings of Democratic congressional candidates and thermometer ratings for the Democratic Party were higher in 1980, 0.36, than in the next three elections. In 1996, the correlation increased markedly to 0.50, which was not matched again until 2012. Even with these occasional downward trends, the overall relationship has largely continued to strengthen as the correlation between thermometer scores for congressional candidates and the party reached a peak of 0.58 in 2020. We see a similar pattern of spikes and slight decreases in the correlation over time between thermometer scores for the Democratic congressional candidate and affect toward liberals. The strength of this relationship across time is sizable, though, as the correlation more than doubled from 0.27 in 1980 to 0.57 in 2020.

Of the three series, the correlation between ratings of Democratic House and presidential candidates comes closest to a monotonic increase. During the 1980s and early 1990s, the correlation between these scores varied between 0.27 and 0.33. From this point onward, though, the correlation largely trends upward and increases from 0.44 in 1996 to 0.59 in 2020. The lack of a consistent upward trend in these scores, like that observed among Republican candidates, is not surprising when we consider the electoral context of this period. First, the magnitude of the incumbency advantage peaked during these years (see Chapter 5), which was due in part to Democrats retaining control of the House despite Republicans winning the White House by comfortable (if not landslide) margins. Under this scenario we would in fact expect a weaker relationship between evaluations of the Democratic House and presidential candidates. Second, the Republicans retook majority control of the House in 1994, and after this point the number of split districts has trended downward (Jacobson and Carson 2020), while competition for control of the House majority has increased (Lee 2016). In this environment, it is increasingly difficult for House candidates, of either party, to build electoral coalitions independent of their respective party's presidential candidate.

## Groups

While shared partisanship can make it easier for the public to link congressional candidates and party leaders or ideological positions, these are not the only cues the public might use when evaluating candidates. The ANES asks respondents to rate a variety of economic and social groups, but we focus for now on those that were included across all or most of the 40-year period for which we have thermometer ratings for House candidates. For Republican candidates, the relevant groups included Big Business, Christian Fundamentalists, and Whites. In the Democratic series we use ratings for Labor Unions, Gays and Lesbians, and Blacks. We report the correlations between group and candidate thermometer scores for each presidential election year from 1980 to 2020 in Figure 7.2.

One of the first points to note is that the relationship between ratings of these groups and House candidates is not as strong as the correlation between congressional candidates and the party stimuli. Next, there has been a general increase over time in the association between affect toward most of these groups and each party's congressional candidates. Interestingly, the most sizable increases appear to be for *social* rather than *economic* groups. For the Republican candidate series, the correlation

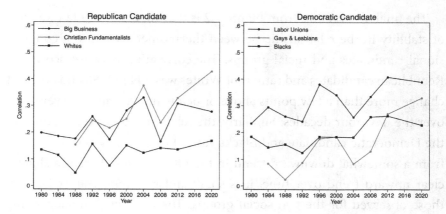

Figure 7.2  House Candidate and Group Feeling Thermometers, 1980–2020

with ratings of Christian Fundamentalists was only 0.15 in 1988, the first year the question was asked, but almost tripled in magnitude by 2020, when it was 0.43. The relationship between thermometer ratings of the Democratic House candidate and affect toward Gays and Lesbians experienced an even more pronounced change, but this has occurred far more recently. From 1984 (the first year the question was asked) to 2008, the correlation between a respondent's ratings ranged from a low of 0.02 in 1992 to a maximum of 0.19 in 2000. By comparison, the correlation between ratings of Christian Fundamentalists and the GOP House candidate was never lower than 0.20 from 1992 onward. Since 2012, though, a respondent's rating of Gays and Lesbians has become a better predictor of her affect toward the Democratic candidate as the correlation increased to 0.27 and 0.33, respectively.

Although the changes are not as pronounced, we do observe the expected increase in correlation between attitudes toward economic groups and congressional candidates. For Republican candidates, the correlation between ratings of Big Business increased from around 0.18 in the 1980s and 1990s to being consistently around 0.30 in the 21st century. In the case of Democratic candidates, the correlation between ratings of Labor Unions and the congressional candidate ranged between 0.23 and 0.29 from 1980 through 1992. By 1996 this increases to 0.38 and has been at that level or slightly higher in most years since.

The final observation from Figure 7.2 is that we uncover a fair amount of stability in the relationship between thermometer ratings of congressional candidates and racial groups. The correlation between scores for Republican candidates and ratings of Whites was 0.14 in 1980 and does not change more than a few points above or below this for most survey years over the next four decades. Similarly, the relationship between ratings of the Democratic candidate and Blacks varies between 0.18 and 0.22, apart from a somewhat downward trend in the 1980s. While there is a slightly clear upward trend over time, it is small and nowhere near as large as those observed for the two social groups. These patterns are surprising given recent research on the racialization of public opinion and politics (Stephens-Dougan 2020; Tesler 2016). Based on these studies, we would expect that attitudes toward racial groups would become more strongly correlated with evaluations of congressional candidates. Indeed, there is compelling evidence of the importance of racial attitudes in candidate evaluations and vote choice (Algara and Hale 2019, 2020; Stephens-Dougan 2020). We suspect that our results reflect our chosen measure, the thermometer scores, rather than being contrary to these past findings. The distribution of the thermometer scores for racial groups has been relatively stable over time, while the candidate thermometer scores were becoming more polarized. Unfortunately, the thermometer scores for each racial group are the only measurements we have that cover an extended time period and ask respondents to rate groups on the same scale as congressional candidates, thus limiting the types of conclusions we can draw from them.

There were a select number of groups the ANES asked respondents to rate at various points that allow for at least some minimal over-time comparisons. The first set of groups we examined were more akin to social groups—Feminists and the Police—and we compared the evaluations of these groups with ratings of the Democratic and Republican candidate, respectively. In 1992, the correlation between thermometer scores for Feminists and the Democratic congressional candidate was 0.26; the correlation for the Police and the GOP House candidate was 0.21. In 2020, which was the next period in which respondents were asked to rate both groups in the same survey, the association between attitudes toward these groups and congressional candidates grew considerably. The correlation between ratings of the Police and the Republican candidate increased to 0.40, while the association between ratings of Feminists and the Democratic House candidate nearly doubled to 0.48.

The next set of groups was economic in nature, the Poor and the Rich. As with the ratings of Big Business and Labor Unions, the relationship between thermometer scores for these groups and congressional candidates was smaller in magnitude than for the corresponding social groups. In 1992, the correlation between ratings of the Poor and the Democratic candidate and the Rich and the GOP candidate were 0.14 and 0.11, respectively. By 2012, the correlations had more than doubled in magnitude—0.30 and 0.26, respectively, as shown in Figure 7.3.

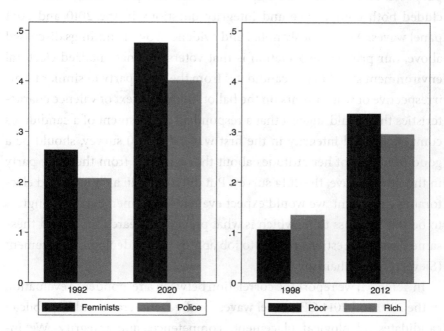

**Figure 7.3** Changes in Correlation of Candidate and Group Feeling Thermometers
NOTE: The black (gray) bars report the correlation between thermometer ratings of the Democratic (Republican) candidate and the rating for each group.

## Candidate Traits

Despite the recognized importance of candidate valence characteristics, there are relatively limited survey data on this topic. Prior studies that explore this question in the context of congressional elections have either relied upon content analysis (McCurley and Mondak 1995; Mondak 1995) or expert surveys (Adams et al. 2011; Buttice and Stone 2012; Stone and Simas 2010). The 2010 Cooperative Election Study (CES), however, included questions that asked respondents to rate each congressional candidate's competence and integrity. Prior studies have utilized these questions to demonstrate that both partisanship and ideological preferences influence perceptions of candidate valence characteristics (Simas 2020; Martin 2022).

Since our interest is how nationalization influences candidate evaluations, however, a one-off survey is not particularly helpful for our purposes. Nevertheless, we can leverage the CES panel study, which included both competence and integrity questions in the 2010 and 2014 panel waves. As previously noted and evidenced by the findings discussed above, our primary expectation is that voters in a nationalized electoral environment should view candidates from the same party in similar terms irrespective of who appears on the ballot. In the context of valence characteristics this would suggest that a respondent's assessment of a candidate's competence and integrity in the first wave, the 2010 survey, should be a good predictor of her attitudes about the candidate from the same party in the second wave, the 2014 survey. Put differently, in a nationalized electoral environment, we would expect evaluations of members of Congress to be stable across time, which is what previous research finds with these same data for questions related to job approval and ideological placement (Sievert and Williamson 2022).

In Table 7.1, we report the correlation between a respondent's evaluation in the 2010 and 2014 CES panel waves for the Democratic and Republican candidates' ideological placement, competence, and integrity. We include the ideological placement question for two key reasons. First, prior research using these same data have uncovered evidence of stability in

Table 7.1 COMPARISON OF CANDIDATE TRAIT EVALUATIONS IN 2010 AND 2014 CES PANEL WAVES

*Democratic Candidate*

| Candidate Evaluation | All | Same Candidate | Different Candidate |
|---|---|---|---|
| Ideological Placement | 0.49 | 0.66 | 0.42 |
| Competence | 0.71 | 0.79 | 0.66 |
| Integrity | 0.69 | 0.78 | 0.63 |

*Republican Candidate*

| Candidate Evaluation | All | Same Candidate | Different Candidate |
|---|---|---|---|
| Ideological Placement | 0.45 | 0.54 | 0.40 |
| Competence | 0.67 | 0.73 | 0.62 |
| Integrity | 0.68 | 0.75 | 0.63 |

NOTE: Cell entries are correlations between a respondent's evaluation of the House candidate across panel waves. The first column reports correlations for all House candidates from the respective parties. The final two columns report the correlations for when the House candidate was the same or different across the two panel waves.

constituents' ideological placement of members of Congress. Second, these scores can provide a benchmark against which to compare evaluations of candidates along the valence dimension. It is well known that both sitting legislators (Hare and Poole 2014) and congressional candidates (Hall 2019; Thomsen 2014) have become more polarized along ideological lines, and we expect this to be reflected in the public's assessment of congressional candidates (Hetherington 2001). Each question asked candidates to rate a given House candidate on a 7-point scale. For the ideological placement question, the possible ratings ranged from Very Liberal (1) to Very Conservative (7), with Middle of the Road serving as the midpoint on the scale. The competence and integrity scales were the same and ran from Extremely Strong (1) to Very Weak (7). The first column of Table 7.1 shows the correlation between evaluations in the 2010 and 2014 survey waves for both Democratic and Republican candidates. We find a strong correspondence between evaluations across time, but the correlations are stronger for the two valence characteristics than for ideological placement. While the correlation in evaluations of both Democratic and Republican candidates is around 0.70 for both competence and integrity, the correlation between panel waves is less than 0.50.

This first set of correlations, however, does not specify who the respondent was evaluating at each wave. We therefore recalculated each correlation based on whether the candidate was the same or different in both survey waves. The second column of Table 7.1 reports these figures for the cases where respondents evaluated the same candidate in both survey waves, and the third column reports the results for when there was a different candidate across the two waves. There is a similar pattern for evaluations of both Democratic and Republican candidates. In general, the relationship between the survey waves is stronger when respondents are asked to evaluate the same candidate. For both Democratic and Republican candidates, these changes are most pronounced with respect to the ideological placement question, while the valence assessments are comparatively closer to those observed in the pooled sample. The substantive implications of these results are that while the public likely sees candidates from the same party in relatively similar ideological terms, there is even greater agreement in evaluations of valence characteristics. Most important, this agreement extends to instances when the candidate changes between waves.

## NATIONALIZER IN CHIEF

Among the various consequences of greater nationalization, one of the most telling is the delicate balancing act that has been required of Republicans in the era of Trump. When Trump was first seeking the Republican nomination in 2015 and 2016, many Republicans initially denounced his candidacy due to his past controversies and proclivity for provocative statements—especially on Twitter. After he defeated Hillary Clinton in 2016, however, many Republicans reluctantly decided to embrace him as the de facto leader of the party. Among Trump's earliest and strongest supporters was House Majority Leader Kevin McCarthy, who had repeatedly defended him in 2016 and continued to do so even after Republicans lost majority control of the House in the 2018 midterms. He continued to support Trump in the aftermath of the 2020 presidential election, claiming that large-scale voter fraud had ultimately cost him the election. McCarthy was one of 126 Republicans in the House who signed an amicus brief in support of *Texas v. Pennsylvania*, trying (and ultimately failing) to get the U.S. Supreme Court to overturn the election results.

McCarthy's support of Trump appeared to waiver after the attack on the U.S. Capitol, which many believe was incited by Trump's speech earlier that day. Two days after the attack, McCarthy held a conference call with other leaders of the House Republican caucus where he criticized Trump's actions and discussed invoking the 25th Amendment to potentially remove him from office. In a follow-up conference call on January 10, McCarthy suggested that Trump should resign rather than endure a long impeachment battle. When an audio version of the phone conversations leaked in April 2022, McCarthy quickly had to engage in damage control after it was suggested that he might no longer be able to lead the Republican Conference. Although as of this writing it appears that McCarthy was able to weather this turn of events, this episode reveals how much influence Trump still holds over Republicans (despite no longer being in office) in a highly nationalized political environment.[3]

The president-centric nature of congressional electoral politics in recent years is not, however, unique to the Trump presidency, nor is it only an issue for Republican legislators. In recent decades, the number of split districts—those where different parties win the most votes in the presidential and congressional contests—has declined substantially and nearly monotonically (Jacobson and Carson 2020). It is now quite rare for a Democratic (Republican) House candidate to win in a district that is carried by the Republican (Democratic) presidential candidate. As we demonstrated in Chapter 5, this means that presidential politics are now an increasingly strong predictor of congressional election outcomes. These patterns are also evidenced in individual-level data as it is increasingly unlikely that a voter will split her ticket between presidential and subpresidential contests (Davis and Mason 2016; Jacobson and Carson 2020; Sievert and McKee 2019).

While past research has thoroughly demonstrated the impact of presidential influence on vote choice and election outcomes, a more nationalized electoral environment has clear implications for candidate evaluations. For example, the declining incumbency advantage in House elections that we document in Chapter 5 and that others have also noted (Jacobson 2015b; Trussler 2021) is theorized to be a result of voters relying more upon national considerations—such as presidential approval or vote choice—rather than candidate-specific attributes, like incumbency. In more general terms, if presidents play an important role in the nationalization of congressional elections, we expect a voter's assessment of a congressional candidate will be highly dependent upon her attitudes toward the president.

A few studies provide preliminary evidence along these lines. There is considerable evidence that presidents and presidential candidates influence attitudes toward and perceptions of the ideological profile of their respective parties (Brasher 2009; Dancey, Tarpey, and Woon 2019; Jacobson 2019b; Sievert and Hinojosa 2022). If the public's understanding of the parties is increasingly president-focused, it follows that candidates from that party will be strongly linked to the president in voters' minds. Indeed, there appears to be a strong connection between the public's perceptions of the president's ideological and issue positions and their views of congressional candidates from the president's party (Amira 2022; Jacobson 2019b). The public's evaluation of a legislator's job performance also bears the imprint of presidential politics (Dancey and Sheagley 2016; Sievert and Williamson 2022).

Although there is considerable evidence that attitudes toward the president correlate with attitudes toward his co-partisans in Congress, there is still much to learn about the mechanisms underlying this relationship. First, to understand how presidents influence candidate evaluations, we need to probe the direction of the relationship. Of particular interest is the potential for a reciprocal relationship between attitudes toward each of these political actors. To do so, we take advantage of recent panel studies by the CES and ANES. Second, we need to compare the president's influence against other potential partisan signals.

## Who Influences Whom?

While there is ample evidence of a relationship between attitudes toward the president and his co-partisans in Congress, we believe it is important to investigate these relationships to better understand their dynamics. We do so by employing recent panel survey studies to assess the temporal linkages between attitudes toward the president and congressional candidates. Our main quantities of interest are the panel study participants' placement of the president and his co-partisan House candidates on the standard 7-point ideological scale.

Our empirical strategy relies on a cross-lagged model, which provides an ideal test for our purposes since it allows us to control for reciprocal relationships without imposing the assumptions required to estimate structural equation models (Carsey and Layman 2006; Finkel 1995). When applied to a two-wave panel study, the cross-lagged model treats attitudes at time $t$ as a function of a respondent's answer to the same question at time $t-1$ as well as her attitudes toward related stimuli. For our purposes, the quantities of interest are the perceived ideological locations of the president and his co-partisans' House candidates. The first two columns of Table 7.2 report the results of these cross-lagged models for placements of the House candidate and president, respectively, for the 2010 to 2012 CES waves, the 2012 to 2014 CES waves, and the 2016 to 2020 ANES waves. For each respective regression model, we have also reported a $F$ test of whether the coefficients for lagged House candidate and presidential placement are equal.

The first point of interest in Table 7.2 is that we find evidence of a reciprocal relationship in two of the three panel waves. The lagged placement of the president, in this case Obama and Trump, is a significant predictor of a respondent's placement of the House candidate from the president's party for both the 2010 to 2012 CES waves and the 2016 to 2020 ANES waves.

*Table 7.2* IDEOLOGICAL PLACEMENT OF HOUSE CANDIDATES AND PRESIDENT ACROSS PANEL WAVES

### CES 2010–2012

| Placement | House | President | House (Same) | House (Different) |
|---|---|---|---|---|
| Obama$_{t-1}$ | 0.17* | 0.73* | 0.06 | 0.26* |
|  | (0.05) | (0.05) | (0.06) | (0.06) |
| Democrat House$_{t-1}$ | 0.40* | 0.11* | 0.56* | 0.30* |
|  | (0.04) | (0.03) | (0.06) | (0.05) |
| N | 4399 | 4399 | 1928 | 2471 |
| $\beta_P = \beta_H (p)$ | 0.00 | 0.00 | 0.00 | 0.70 |

### CES 2012–2014

| Placement | House | President | House (Same) | House (Different) |
|---|---|---|---|---|
| Obama$_{t-1}$ | 0.27* | 0.78* | 0.24* | 0.37* |
|  | (0.04) | (0.03) | (0.06) | (0.05) |
| Democrat House$_{t-1}$ | 0.43* | -0.01 | 0.44* | 0.34* |
|  | (0.03) | (0.03) | (0.05) | (0.04) |
| N | 4648 | 4648 | 2638 | 2010 |
| $\beta_P = \beta_H (p)$ | 0.02 | 0.00 | 0.02 | 0.68 |

### ANES 2016–2020

| Placement | House | President | House (Same) | House (Different) |
|---|---|---|---|---|
| Trump$_{t-1}$ | 0.11* | 0.32* | 0.08 | 0.13* |
|  | (0.02) | (0.03) | (0.04) | (0.03) |
| Republican House$_{t-1}$ | 0.29* | 0.17* | 0.34* | 0.26* |
|  | (0.03) | (0.04) | (0.05) | (0.04) |
| N | 1804 | 1804 | 642 | 1162 |
| $\beta_P = \beta_H (p)$ | 0.00 | 0.00 | 0.00 | 0.02 |

NOTE: Cell entries are OLS regression coefficients, and robust standard errors are reported in parentheses. The first column reports results for the ideological placement of House candidates from the president's party. The second column reports results for the ideological placement of the president or presidential candidate. The final two columns report the results for when the House candidate was the same or different across the two panel waves. In the final row of each panel analysis, we report the *p* value for a test of the equality of the regression estimates for lagged presidential and House candidate placement. * p < 0.05.

The same is true for lagged placement of the House candidate in the model that predicts placement of the president in the current period. Taken together, these results suggest that rather than being a unidirectional relationship with the causal arrow pointing away from the president, the public's assessment of House candidates can also influence perceptions of the president's ideological location.

While there is evidence of a reciprocal relationship, these results also suggest a fair amount of stability in evaluations. We can see this by examining the magnitude of the lagged placement for both the House candidate and president, which is always larger in size than the estimate for the lagged placement of the other politician. In the CES panel studies, the lagged estimate for placements of Obama were between 0.7 and 0.8 points larger in size. For placement of the House candidate the differences are around 0.2 points. The difference drops markedly in both sets of models in the ANES panel study with Trump, which is not surprising given that his positions defied many tenets of Republican Party orthodoxy (Amira 2022; Barber and Pope 2019). Furthermore, these differences are all statistically meaningful as we can reject the null hypothesis of coefficient equality in each of the specifications.

These initial cross-lagged models, however, do not account for whether the House candidate being evaluated was the same across the two survey waves. Substantively, this means that although respondents are evaluating the same president across survey waves, at least some participants are comparing different House candidates across the two periods. As our analysis and results in Table 7.1 indicate, this may not necessarily be an issue in a nationalized electoral environment if voters use the same criteria to evaluate all candidates from the same party. To better understand the mechanisms through which presidents drive evaluations of congressional candidates, however, it is prudent to incorporate this information into our analysis. We reestimated the model predicting placement of the House candidate for cases where it was the same or different candidate across the two survey waves. These results are reported in the third and fourth columns of Table 7.2.

The lagged placement of presidential ideology does not have a significant effect on placement of the House candidate in two of the three models where the House candidate is the same between the two waves. The one exception is the 2012 to 2014 CES panel, but even then we find that greater weight is given to the lagged perception of the House candidate's ideology. When we focus on cases where the House candidate changes between panel waves, however, we find that perceptions of the president and former House candidate are given similar weight in the CES panel study. Since these panels are from successive elections, it suggests that when voters are asked to rate a new candidate, their evaluations rely on cues from both the president and former House candidates. In the ANES panel study, though, we find that attitudes toward congressional candidates are still given about twice as much weight as are assessments of Trump. As we suggested earlier, these results may simply be a function of Trump's unique and somewhat unorthodox set of policy positions and priorities. It is still telling that it is only in cases where the House candidate changed between survey waves that the public uses their views of the president when evaluating House candidates. Overall, these findings have important implications for co-partisan challengers or open-seat candidates who will find it more difficult to distinguish themselves from the president.

## Presidents and Partisan Endorsements

With respect to candidate evaluations, the president is most likely to play a key role through the endorsement of candidates. One approach, then, would be to compare candidates who were and were not endorsed by the president, but there are potential methodological limits to this approach (Amira 2022). For our purposes, the biggest limitation is that it does not help us to distinguish the influence of the president from other potential competing partisan cues. Indeed, one of the key challenges in identifying the unique effect of the president on public attitudes is to distinguish presidential cues from other partisan signals (Barber and Pope 2019; Jacobson 2019b; Nicholson 2011; Sievert and Hinojosa 2022). Since partisanship serves as an important referent for political candidates (Rahn 1993), it is necessary to compare an endorsement from the president against those from other partisan actors. We do this through a survey experiment, which allows us to manipulate whether a candidate is endorsed by the president or another partisan group.[4]

Each respondent in our survey was asked to read a short vignette about a congressional candidate that included background information about our hypothetical candidate's professional and political experience. We randomly assigned participants to one of four endorsement categories: President Trump, President Biden, the National Republican Congressional Committee, or the Democratic Congressional Campaign Committee. We chose the House campaign committees as our alternative partisan endorser because they both actively endorse candidates and provide key resources to candidates (Roberts, Smith, and Treul 2016). After reading the vignette, each respondent was asked to answer a series of questions about the candidate. The first task was to place the candidate on the standard 7-point ideological scale. Next, respondents were asked to rate their favorability toward the candidate, which could take values from Very Unfavorable (1) to Very Favorable (5), with Neither Favorable nor Unfavorable serving as the midpoint. Last, each respondent assessed the candidate's qualifications to hold office along an ordinal scale of Weak (1), Fair (2), and Strong (3).[5]

Since our interest is the impact of a presidential cue relative to a competing partisan cue, we limit our analysis to a comparison of the effect of a Biden (Trump) endorsement against a DCCC (NRCC) endorsement. In Figure 7.4, we report the results of a difference of means test that compares ratings of the candidate endorsed by the president with attitudes toward the candidate endorsed by one of the congressional party campaign committees. A presidential endorsement serves as a meaningful cue for the public about a congressional candidate's ideology. A Democratic House candidate who is endorsed by President Biden is seen as more liberal than one who is endorsed by the party campaign organization. We find the mirror opposite effect for Republican candidates, with a Trump endorsement resulting in a candidate being viewed as more conservative.

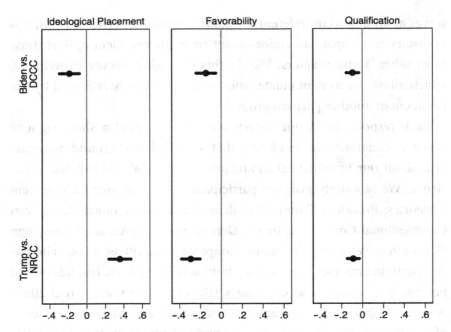

**Figure 7.4** Effects of Endorsement Type by Endorser Partisanship
NOTE: Each dot denotes the difference in means between a candidate endorsed by the president and one supported by his party's respective congressional campaign committee, while the lines report 95 percent confidence intervals.

It is interesting to note that the magnitude of the effect is almost double that observed for Democratic candidates, differences of 0.37 and –0.19, respectively. These results add to the growing body of evidence that Trump's presidency redefined how the public understands the meaning of the conservative brand (Amira 2022; Barber and Pope 2019; Hopkins and Noel 2022; Lewis 2021) but also provide important evidence about the influence of Trump relative to other recent presidents.

Our results for candidate favorability and qualification show how a presidential endorsement can undermine a candidate in the public's eyes. When respondents were told of a Biden or Trump endorsement, they were more likely to view the candidate less favorably and as being less qualified. As with ideological placement, Trump has a larger impact on candidate evaluations than does Biden. A congressional candidate endorsed by Trump is rated roughly –0.30 points less favorably than is a candidate endorsed by the NRCC. For a Democratic candidate, however, the penalty of a presidential endorsement is only a −0.15-point drop in favorability. With respect to candidate qualifications, we find that both the Democratic and Republican candidates are viewed as slightly less qualified, a 0.09-point decrease, when they are endorsed by the president instead of their party's congressional campaign committee.

While these initial results make it clear that presidents influence how the public views congressional candidates, we believe that the president's co-partisans should respond differently to this cue than do individuals who identify with the opposition party. First, the public's evaluation of presidential politics and job performance has become highly polarized along partisan lines, with co-partisans uniformly supporting the president and the out party consistently in opposition (Donovan et al. 2020; Jacobson 2019b; Sievert and Williamson 2018). Second, and relatedly, a voter's attitudes toward and response to candidates are increasingly driven by her affect toward the party, with negative affect driving evaluations more than positive affect (Abramowitz and Webster 2016; Bankert 2020). Based on these considerations, we expect the opposition to be more responsive to a presidential endorsement than the president's co-partisans. We test this by estimating a series of regression models where the dependent variables are the three survey questions discussed in Figure 7.4 and the predictors are an indicator for how presidential endorsement interacted with respondent partisanship. As before, we subset the data so that we compare the effect of a Biden endorsement against one from the DCCC and a Trump-backed candidate to one supported by the NRCC. For each model, we calculate the marginal effect of a presidential endorsement by respondent partisanship and report these quantities in Figure 7.5.

The first panel of Figure 7.5 provides our findings for views on the candidate's ideological placement. Among the respondents who were asked to evaluate a Democratic candidate, only Republicans viewed a Biden endorsement (black dots) as a sign that the candidate was more liberal than one who was supported by the DCCC. For the Republican candidate, we find that all partisans and Independents viewed a candidate backed by Trump (gray dots) as more conservative than one endorsed by

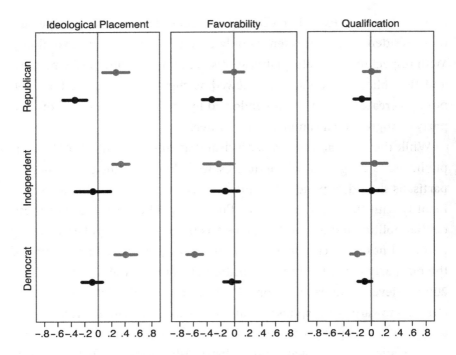

**Figure 7.5** Marginal Effect of Presidential Endorsement by Partisanship
NOTE: The black (gray) dots denote the marginal effect of a Biden (Trump) endorsement on candidate evaluations by respondent partisanship, while the lines report 95 percent confidence intervals.

the NRCC. The marginal effect of a Trump endorsement is larger among Democrats, a 0.41-unit increase in conservatism, than among Republicans, a 0.27-point increase. While the difference is small, the magnitude of these effects still fits our general expectation that the out party will be more responsive to presidential involvement in congressional races than will the president's co-partisans.

A presidential statement of support has the expected effect on favorability ratings across partisans. For the Democratic candidate, only Republican identifiers offer consistently more negative assessments of the presidentially backed candidate, a −0.32-unit decrease in favorability. We once again find that Trump's endorsement leads to both a substantively larger and more consistent decrease in support. Both Independents and Democrats respond less favorably to a candidate with Trump's backing, a roughly −0.2- and −0.6-unit change, respectively. In total, these results suggest that Trump may be even more polarizing than his predecessors and successor. Finally, we find substantively weaker but theoretically consistent effects of presidential support on perceptions of a candidate's qualifications. Both the Democratic and Republican candidates are viewed as weakly more qualified among Republicans, 0.13- and 0.20-unit decreases, respectively, when endorsed by the president instead of the congressional campaign committees. These patterns indicate that much of the drop in perceptions of candidate quality are driven by out-partisans who react negatively to the president. We do, however, find that Democratic identifiers were also more likely to view a Biden-supported candidate as marginally less qualified (p = 0.06) than one with the endorsement of the DCCC. These findings may reflect Biden's comparatively low standing within his own party compared to other recent presidents.[6]

## SUMMARY

We began this chapter by asking whether the public has begun viewing congressional candidates from each party in increasingly uniform terms. Based on the analyses reported here, we believe the answer to that question is a firm yes. As nationalization has increased, so too has the linkage between candidates and party-aligned actors, which includes not only party leaders but also social and economic groups. Furthermore, Americans increasingly evaluate individual candidates' ideology and qualifications based on cues from other partisans, which creates greater homogeneity in opinion toward the Democratic and Republican parties. Taken as a whole, the findings reported in this chapter provide us with substantial evidence of the recent increase in nationalization being driven by individual attitudes and vote choice and reaching levels not seen since the use of the party ballot.

One of the more important takeaways from this chapter is that it adds nuance to our understanding of how the linkage between congressional and presidential candidates fuels the nationalization of elections. Namely, presidential effects vary based on different groups of candidates. Those who do not have as much of an established reputation within their district, such as challengers and open-seat candidates, have a more difficult time distinguishing themselves from their co-partisan presidential candidate counterparts. Importantly, our analysis depicts former president Trump as uniquely influential in terms of redefining both the conservative brand and the power of the presidency more broadly. What remains to be seen is if Trump continues to stand out among his predecessors, or if increased nationalization will continue to enable presidents to influence how voters perceive congressional candidates and who they ultimately vote for.

# 8

# Contextualizing Nationalization

*The 2020 Elections*

The Alabama U.S. Senate special election to fill Jeff Sessions's vacant seat after he was appointed to be the U.S. attorney general in 2017 was full of surprises. The Republican nominee, former Alabama Supreme Court chief justice Roy Moore, was a divisive figure, having twice been removed from the court for judicial misconduct. The Democratic nominee, Doug Jones, was a former federal prosecutor most noted for prosecuting the Ku Klux Klan members responsible for bombing the Sixteenth Street Baptist Church in 1963. Given Alabama's strong Republican leanings, it seemed like Moore's race to lose. In the waning days of the campaign, however, stories came to light that credibly accused Moore of sexual misconduct with minors.[1] These reports stirred immense controversy and ultimately culminated in Alabama's senior U.S. senator, Republican Richard Shelby, publicly stating that he would write in a different name rather than supporting Moore and encouraged other Republicans voters to do the same.[2] Paired with massive mobilization and turnout from Black voters, especially women, Jones was able to win the election by a slim 1.6 percent margin.[3]

Once seated, some pundits questioned whether Jones could retain his seat in the 2020 election and wondered if he should moderate his positions or even try to engage in bipartisan behavior.[4] Rather than concede the election to pursue more liberal policies and work against the Republican

*Nationalized Politics.* Jamie L. Carson, Joel Sievert, and Ryan D. Williamson, Oxford University Press.
© Oxford University Press 2024. DOI: 10.1093/oso/9780197669655.003.0008

president, Jones cultivated a clearly moderate, bipartisan record during his three years in the Senate. His common refrain on the campaign trail was "I will continue to be an independent voice for Alabama who cares more about the issues that unite us than those that divide us," and he adhered to his word.[5] Jones's legislative style did not go unnoticed by his Senate colleagues—even those on the opposite side of the aisle acknowledged his record of bipartisanship. Tennessee Republican senator Lamar Alexander said of Jones, "I like senators who try to work across party lines. . . . [H]e votes independent of his own party."[6]

By almost all accounts, Jones ran an aggressive campaign in his 2020 bid for a full term, and his reelection prospects should, in theory, have been aided by his next challenger, former college football coach Tommy Tuberville. Tuberville had no elective experience, considerably less money, and his campaign was relatively devoid of substance.[7] Furthermore, he was not a native Alabamian, nor had he lived in the state for many of the previous years. Tuberville refused to debate Jones or answer questions from the media, which allowed Jones to largely dominate the narrative leading up to the election. Tuberville's primary message to voters was that he would support President Trump, and he even went so far as to declare, "God sent us Donald Trump."[8]

The 2020 Alabama U.S. Senate race provided an interesting test of the extent of nationalization in the context of the election: an experienced, well-funded, moderate incumbent versus an inexperienced ideologue challenger. As one political consultant commented in the days leading up the election, "Jones can run the perfect race and still lose by 7 points."[9] One Alabama voter went so far as to say, with respect to Jones, "[H]e's been responsive to us farmers, but we're not going to vote for him."[10] In short, Jones's experience, strategy, and resources could not make up for the fact that he was not a Republican in the consistently Republican state of Alabama. After the ballots were tabulated, Tuberville prevailed. Nevertheless, it is important to note that Jones outperformed Democratic presidential candidate Joe Biden in the state. Though Jones received only 39.6 percent of the vote in Alabama, that is 3.2 percentage points higher than the percentage of the vote won by Biden. Jones was able to win over tens of thousands of Trump voters, but not nearly enough to change the outcome of the election.

This anecdote is illustrative of two important points that we will discuss in this chapter. First, the 2020 elections were highly nationalized, which continues a trend that has characterized elections in recent decades. Second, despite a more nationalized electoral environment, individual candidates can still influence voters' choices, which can be consequential in particularly close contests.

## NATIONALIZATION OF THE 2020 SENATE ELECTIONS

Both pundits and scholars argued that the highly contentious 2020 elections would serve as a referendum on incumbent president Trump (Jacobson 2021). In this section, we analyze the ties between the presidential vote and vote shares in accompanying House and Senate races. As previously mentioned, the 2016 elections saw complete convergence (i.e., no partisan splits) between presidential and senatorial races. In other words, each state won by Democratic candidate Clinton also saw the Democratic senatorial candidate win, and each state won by Republican candidate Trump witnessed a Republican senatorial candidate victory. That trend largely continued in the 2020 elections. Again, there were no partisan splits between presidential and senatorial contests, save one exception in Maine, depicted in Figure 8.1.[11]

Figure 8.1 represents the two-party vote share earned by the Democratic candidate in each state holding a Senate election. These vote shares are correlated at 0.93. Again, only one state witnessed candidates from different parties win statewide: Senator Susan Collins and presidential-candidate Joe Biden in the state of Maine. However, neither candidate won by an overwhelming margin; both won with less than 55 percent of the vote. More broadly, Democratic incumbents outperformed Democratic challengers by an average of 57.1 percent to 41.5 percent. Though this difference is statistically significant, it is comparable to the share of the vote won by Democratic presidential candidate Biden. In the same 11 states

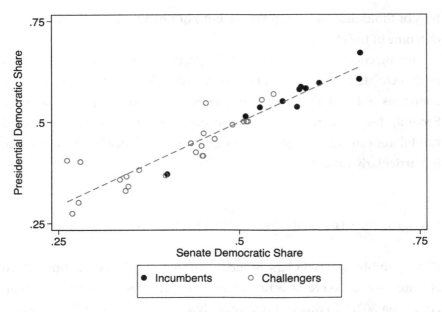

**Figure 8.1** Democratic Share of Presidential and Senate Votes in 2020 Elections

with Democratic incumbents, Biden won 55.8 percent of the vote, and in the same 20 states featuring challenges to Republican incumbents, Biden won 43.2 percent of the vote. This suggests that individual characteristics exerted little effect on election results. On average, Biden's name recognition may have allowed him to run ahead of Democratic challengers, and incumbency may have allowed senators to run ahead of Biden, but in both cases that difference is less than 2 percentage points.

States that were competitive at the presidential level also featured competitive Senate elections. In Arizona, Georgia, Michigan, and North Carolina, the winning candidates at both the Senate and presidential level received less than 52 percent of the two-party votes, which illustrates how the strength of partisanship within the state was determinative of election outcomes in 2020. While there were differences across these races with respect to candidate characteristics such as incumbency, campaign style and resources, or personal characteristics, candidates could expect to receive a certain percentage of the vote based on partisanship alone. Furthermore, the close correspondence between presidential and senatorial vote shares suggests that it was difficult to induce a large enough change in that baseline to alter the outcome of an election.

There were, however, some notable exceptions to the general trend of candidates from the same party taking the statewide vote in both the presidential and Senate races. As previously mentioned, Republican senator Collins was able to retain her seat despite Democratic presidential candidate Biden winning the state's Electoral College votes. Collins was viewed as one of the most vulnerable Senate incumbents leading up to the 2020 elections, and she faced Sara Gideon, who was the speaker of the Maine House of Representatives. Gideon's candidacy was endorsed by former president Obama, presidential candidate Biden, six sitting U.S. senators, including vice presidential candidate Kamala Harris, and Chellie Pingree, who represented Maine's First Congressional District in the U.S. House. The total spending in the contest neared $180 million, but the outpouring of campaign funds was not enough to defeat Collins. Maine voters were inundated with ads and eventually grew disaffected by the effort to remove the 24-year incumbent. One was quoted as saying, "What I really think happened was that the national Democratic Party was too heavy-handed," and another stated, "The approach on the ads and campaigning was disgusting enough that I didn't want to vote for the person anymore, even though I agreed with the policy stances."[12]

Though there were notable exceptions like this one in Maine, the 2020 election largely illustrates how nationalization is the new "normal" and individual-level characteristics rarely serve to shape election outcomes—even in statewide races (Sievert and McKee 2019). In short, the 2020 U.S. Senate elections were consistent with other recent work on the nationalization of elections. Specifically, the incumbency advantage associated with members of Congress has diminished considerably since the era of more localized elections in the mid-20th century (Carson, Sievert, and Williamson 2020), and support for the presidential candidate has become increasingly predictive of Senate vote shares when the two represent the same political party. Additionally, Sievert and Williamson (2022) highlight how individual opinions of senators are much more stable over the course of their six-year terms—contrary to previous research—and suggest increased nationalization and polarization can explain why. Collectively, these works illustrate the devaluation of individual characteristics, including incumbency, and the increased weight of the presidential vote—both of which are evident in the 2020 elections.

## NATIONALIZATION OF THE 2020 HOUSE ELECTIONS

In the weeks leading up to the 2020 elections, Democrats were expected to expand their majority in the House of Representatives, but ultimately ended up losing seats despite maintaining their overall majority. Many moderate Democrats (largely in competitive districts) lost their reelection bids, and those who survived grew upset with their more progressive colleagues. This culminated in a heated exchange within the caucus. Virginia representative Abigail Spanberger forcefully stated, "We need to not ever use the word 'socialist' or 'socialism' ever again.... We lost good members because of that." Oregon representative Kurt Schrader stated, "When [voters] see the far left that gets all the news media attention, they get scared. They're very afraid that this will become a supernanny state, and their ability to do things on their own is going to be taken away."[13] These sentiments were echoed by several other moderate Democratic House members. In discussing attack ads painting him as a radical leftist, Cameron Webb, an unsuccessful Democratic House candidate from Virginia, said, "But that did shift the conversation. And what it did is it brought more national discourse into our race here in the 5th as opposed to focusing on local issues."[14] In short, Republicans were able to tie moderate Democratic candidates to a more liberal national brand, which eventually shrank the size of the Democratic majority.

Like the Senate races, the 2020 House elections also proved to be highly nationalized affairs, as illustrated by the correlation of votes in Democratic congressional and presidential races in Figure 8.2. These vote totals are highly correlated at 0.98. Of the 435 House races, only 16 districts were won by Biden (Trump) and the Republican (Democratic) House candidate. Furthermore, Democrats seeking seats in the U.S. House ran

Contextualizing Nationalization

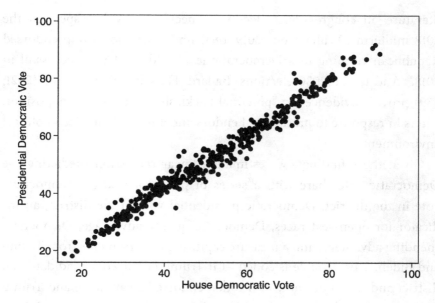

**Figure 8.2** Democratic Share of Presidential and House Votes in 2020 Elections

ahead of Biden in 161 races, while Biden ran ahead in 274 districts, which suggests that presidents are substantial drivers of nationalized vote choice. This further demonstrates the highly nationalized nature of congressional elections in recent years.

## ENDORSEMENTS IN THE 2020 ELECTIONS

In a highly nationalized environment, an endorsement from the president is likely to be superfluous to partisan-aligned districts and insufficient or even harmful in non-partisan-aligned districts. This has obvious consequences for election outcomes. As we demonstrated in Chapter 7, endorsements can shape how voters view individual candidates. Furthermore, by eliminating the endorsement as a tool to curry favor with members of Congress, this also speaks to presidents' ability to shape the legislative agenda and realize their policy goals. Therefore, we now discuss the evolving nature of presidential endorsements by building off recent literature on congressional elections. Specifically, with respect to the 2018 midterms, Williamson (2019, 683) finds that "no Trump-endorsed Republican running in a Democratic leaning district was successful in 2018." And in the 2020 elections, Ballard, Hassell, and Heseltine (2021, 459) provide evidence for "potential backlash effects among opposition voters in response to presidential endorsement in a nationalized political environment."

Given these findings, we estimate a linear regression predicting the Democratic vote share with a series of predictors: lagged Democratic vote in the district, Democratic presidential vote in the district, an indicator for open-seat races, Democratic quality advantage, Democratic spending advantage, and a measure capturing endorsements from Trump and Biden. This variable is coded –1 if Trump endorsed a candidate in a district and Biden did not, +1 if Biden endorsed a candidate and Trump did not, and 0 if both presidential candidates either endorsed candidates directly competing against each other or endorsed neither candidate in a given election. The results of this model are presented in Table 8.1.

A few striking patterns emerge; most notably, endorsements do not seem to have been able to induce a measurable effect on the Democratic share of the two-party vote. Additionally, financial competition exerts a statistically significant but relatively small substantively significant effect. For every $1 million a Democratic candidate spends over their Republican opponent, they are expected to earn less than one-quarter of a percent of the vote in return. Moving from the lowest value on this variable (spending $33 million less) to the highest (spending $6 million more) results in a predicted Democratic vote share of 43.3 percent to only 52.0 percent. Indeed, all else being equal, a Democratic House candidate would have been expected to win a majority of votes in 2020 even at a $3 million spending disadvantage. Conversely, the Democratic presidential vote share was a noticeably strong predictor of Democratic House candidate performance in 2020, even more so than the Democratic share of the vote in the 2018 midterm elections. Consistent with the logic in Chapters 5 and 7, we also see no significant difference between incumbent-contested and open-seat races in 2020 after accounting for other factors.

Table 8.1 PREDICTED 2020 HOUSE DEMOCRATIC VOTE SHARE

|  | Estimated (S.E.) |
|---|---|
| Lagged Democratic Vote | 0.10* |
|  | (0.02) |
| Democratic Presidential Vote | 0.86* |
|  | (0.02) |
| Open Seats | 0.19 |
|  | (0.44) |
| Democratic Quality Advantage | 1.29* |
|  | (0.23) |
| Democratic Spending Advantage | 0.22* |
|  | (0.05) |
| Endorsements | −0.25 |
|  | (0.30) |
| Intercept | 0.90 |
|  | (0.75) |
| N | 406 |
| $R^2$ | 0.973 |

NOTE: Cell entries are coefficient estimates from an OLS regression model with presented with standard errors in parentheses. *p<0.05.

What, then, do we make of two presidential candidates actively endorsing congressional candidates with no discernible impact on the election outcomes? These findings are likely driven by where presidential candidates decided to offer endorsements. In Senate races, Trump endorsed 23 candidates out of the 35 possible. These are broken down by race ratings from the Cook Political Report in Table 8.2.[15] As this table illustrates, most of Trump's endorsements for Senate races came in contests Republicans were already expected to win. For the House elections, Trump's endorsement pattern initially appears somewhat different. Limiting our analysis to only the 91 races Cook rated as competitive, we see Trump much more active in races where Democrats were favored. However, these are only 59 of the former president's 145 endorsements, which indicates that most of his endorsements occurred in districts where they were unlikely to sway the outcome. Of the 86 endorsements not listed

*Table 8.2* TRUMP ENDORSEMENTS BY RACE RATING

|  | Republican Favored | Toss-up | Democratic Favored |
|---|---|---|---|
|  |  | *Senate* |  |
| Trump Endorsement | 13 | 6 | 6 |
| No Endorsement | 1 | 1 | 8 |
|  |  | *House* |  |
| Trump Endorsement | 15 | 16 | 28 |
| No Endorsement | 13 | 10 | 9 |

NOTE: Ratings provided by Cook Political Report.

in Table 8.2, 80 of them went to candidates running in districts that were already held by Republicans.

To investigate this relationship more systematically, we estimate a logistic outcome of presidential candidate endorsements in House races. The outcome is coded 1 if Trump or Biden offered an endorsement in the race, and 0 otherwise. We include the same controls as the model presented in Table 8.1 except for the endorsement variable. Instead, we include an indicator variable denoting whether the presidential candidate's opponent offered an endorsement in a given election. The results are presented in Table 8.3.

The patterns are consistent across each of the 2020 presidential candidates. Both Biden and Trump were more likely to offer an endorsement to candidates running in highly partisan districts. In districts where Biden received 25 percent of the vote, Trump's predicted probability of endorsing a candidate is 75 percent, compared to Biden's 3 percent. Conversely, in districts where Biden received 75 percent of the vote, Trump's likelihood of endorsing a candidate drops to 6 percent, while Biden's rises to 29 percent. The presidential candidates were also more likely to weigh in on races where the other did so. Trump's predicted probability of offering an endorsement in the same district as Biden is 51 percent, compared to 33 percent in other districts. Biden offered fewer endorsements, but his probability of doing so nearly tripled in races where Trump was also active (5 percent compared to 13 percent). Together, this

Table 8.3 PREDICTED PRESIDENTIAL CANDIDATE ENDORSEMENT IN HOUSE RACES

|  | Trump Endorsed Estimate (Standard Error) | Biden Endorsed Estimate (Standard Error) |
|---|---|---|
| Lagged Democratic Vote | −0.03 (0.02) | −0.03 (0.02) |
| Democratic Presidential Vote | −0.08** (0.02) | 0.06** (0.03) |
| Open Seats | 0.79* (0.40) | 1.11** (0.45) |
| Democratic Quality Advantage | 0.29 (0.22) | −0.59* (0.32) |
| Democratic Spending Advantage | 0.12** (0.06) | 0.07 (0.09) |
| Opposition Endorsed | 1.07** (0.42) | 1.06** (0.47) |
| Intercept | 4.58** (0.78) | −4.91** (1.12) |
| N | 406 | 406 |
| Log-likelihood | −195.87 | −100.66 |

NOTE: Cell entries are estimates from a logistic regression with standard errors in parentheses, *p < 0.10, **p < 0.05.

indicates that endorsements were largely in races where such intervention was superfluous or negated by the other candidate. There do appear to be some additional strategic calculations underlying the decision to endorse a congressional candidate. Both candidates were more likely to endorse candidates running in open seats (an 11-percentage-point increase in Biden's predicted probability and a 14-percentage-point increase in Trump's). Biden and Trump were also more involved when their co-partisan was at some sort of disadvantage. Biden was more likely to endorse a candidate when the Republican had a quality advantage, and Trump was more likely to do so when the Democrat had a spending advantage.

In Senate contests, Trump once again focused on races already favoring his party. Of the 11 Senate races that featured a Democratic incumbent, Trump endorsed a Republican candidate in only 4 elections. In all 4, the final election outcome was consistent with the pre-election expectations based on the Cook Political Report race ratings. Furthermore, none of the seven races rated by Cook as "toss-ups" featured a Democratic incumbent. Although Trump endorsed the GOP candidate in six of those seven races, Democrats won two of the seven (both in Georgia). The other five competitive races that featured Republican incumbents were either in states where Democrats rarely win statewide elections (Iowa, Montana, and South Carolina) or in states that are fairly competitive (Maine and North Carolina). Overall, it appears that endorsements were not determinative of 2020 Senate election outcomes, as Republican candidates were already tied to Trump through nationalization.

In the House races, only 21 districts split their vote between House and presidential candidates. Of these 21 districts, 10 were won by Biden and 11 were won by Trump. Trump endorsed a candidate in 8 of these 11 districts. Although Trump was able to carry these districts, his endorsement was not sufficient to propel candidates down-ballot to victory. Indeed, his involvement in the race could have countermobilized the opposition and instead cost the Republican Party those seats in Congress. In the 10 split Biden districts, Trump endorsed only 4 of the candidates, which is consistent with the idea that endorsements were targeted at favorable districts and suggests these Republicans may have triumphed despite Trump's presence on the ballot. It is also noteworthy that the split districts did not see overwhelming margins for either candidate. Of the 21 splits, 13 saw the winning candidate prevail with less than 55 percent of the vote.

## NATIONALIZATION AND ACCOUNTABILITY

As discussed in earlier chapters, the level of nationalization seen in recent election cycles rivals that of the outcomes seen in the 1800s. However, the key difference between these two time periods is what facilitated that nationalization. Institutional factors made it difficult, or even impossible at times, for voters to split their tickets throughout much of the 19th century. Numerous electoral reforms have allowed voters to split their tickets and prioritize local issues since then, but many are simply choosing not to do so given the increased emphasis on national politics. One consequence of this behavior is that accountability looks very different under these high levels of nationalization.

To illustrate this point, we discuss the effects of the COVID-19 global pandemic on vote choice in the 2020 presidential election. By Election Day in 2020, over 231,000 Americans had died because of COVID-19, according to Johns Hopkins University. In March 2020, when a state of emergency was declared, Trump's approval rating was 49 percent, according to Gallup—tying the highest level it had been during his term in office. His approval steadily shrank as the pandemic worsened, reaching a low of 38 percent in June 2020. However, as the election grew near, his approval rating started to improve. In the last Gallup poll before the election, his approval rating sat at 46 percent, on par with his approval on Inauguration Day of 45 percent.

In reporting after the election, NPR found, "People living in counties that went 60% or higher for Trump in November 2020 had 2.73 times the death rates of those that went for Biden."[16] Furthermore, despite vaccines becoming widely available in 2021, this report showed that "[t]he higher the vote share for Trump, the lower the vaccination rate." From this, we see that Trump's approval remained remarkably stable despite a deadly pandemic that many argued had been greatly mismanaged by the president and his administration. In fact, those most negatively affected by his actions and the pandemic were counterintuitively *more* likely to support him. This is further documented by Jacobson (2020), who illustrated the extremely polarized attitude of partisans toward Trump's handling of the pandemic. By September 2020, fewer than 10 percent of Democrats approved of Trump's management of the situation compared to over 80 percent of Republicans.

Based on an analysis of the effects of COVID cases and deaths on the 2020 presidential and congressional elections, Carson, Hardin, and Hitefield (2021) confirmed that Trump and congressional Republicans did better in parts of the country that had higher rates of COVID cases and deaths prior to the election. They hypothesized that COVID deaths might operate similarly to casualties in wartime leading to reduced electoral margins for both the president and members of Congress. This would be consistent with Gartner, Segura, and Barratt (2003, 467) who in their analysis of the Vietnam War conclude, "Incumbents from states that experience higher casualties receive a smaller percentage of the vote." Kriner and Shen (2007), in their analysis of the war in Iraq, find that even though the number of casualties was lower than in some other militarized disputes, Republican Senate candidates still suffered electorally in 2006. With respect to the presidency, Karol and Miguel (2007, 633) argue that "were it not for the approximately 10,000 U.S. dead and wounded by Election Day, Bush would have won nearly 2% more of the national popular vote, carrying several additional states and winning decisively."

Despite this, Carson, Harden, and Hitefield (2021) did not find such an effect with respect to the 2020 elections. Instead, it appears that Republican voters rallied around the president *despite* the ongoing pandemic, much as we see a "rally around the flag" effect during times of war or crisis. This effect seemed to be largely confined to Republican voters, however, as Democrats attributed the problems with COVID, the economy, and race relations, among many others, to the former president (Aldrich et al. 2022).

The preceding discussion could help explain the underperformance seen by Democratic House candidates in the 2020 elections. According to *The Economist*, Democrats were expected to win between 227 and 264 seats, but ultimately won only 222, to barely retain their majority.[17] By nationalizing the election around the pandemic response, the Republican Party and its candidates were not electorally punished for the deaths seen across the country. Instead, many Democratic candidates who may have been buoyed by such a catastrophe in a period of more localized politics (as in the middle of the 20th century) were tied to policies implemented by national Democratic figures like California governor Gavin Newsome and New York governor Andrew Cuomo, which were unpopular in more competitive and Republican-leaning districts.

## NATIONALIZATION IN THE 2021 GUBERNATORIAL ELECTIONS

As discussed in earlier chapters, nationalization is not limited to federal offices. In the immediate aftermath of the 2020 elections, gubernatorial elections in Virginia and New Jersey would garner immense attention. In Virginia, governors are prohibited from seeking consecutive terms, leaving incumbent Ralph Northam off the ballot, and therefore pitted the former Democratic governor Terry McAuliffe against the once co-CEO of the Carlyle Group, Glenn Youngkin, as the Republican candidate. A Republican had not held the governor's office since the end of Bob McDonnell's tenure in 2014, both of the state's senators are Democrats, and the state has offered its Electoral College votes to the Democratic nominee for president in every election since 2008. Despite these trends, Youngkin emerged victorious with 50.6 percent of the vote.

The race proved to be highly nationalized, as one might expect. In the first debate, the candidates sparred over President Biden's vaccine mandate for certain sectors of the workforce, a controversial Texas abortion bill, climate change, elections, and the economy. During the discussion of the Texas Heartbeat Act (which was the most restrictive abortion ban in the country at the time, prohibiting abortions starting around six weeks), McAuliffe tried to frame Youngkin as someone who wanted to completely ban abortion. However, Youngkin said he would not sign a similar bill into law in Virginia if he became governor. He further identified himself as "pro-life" but supported exceptions for cases involving rape and incest and advocated for a ban on most abortions after 20 weeks. During their discussion of the election, McAuliffe noted that former president Trump endorsed Youngkin and called him a "Trump wannabe." In response, Youngkin emphasized that he believed the 2020 election was not fraudulent, that Biden was "our president," and that he would concede if he lost the election.[18]

As this debate shows, McAuliffe tried to tie Youngkin to unpopular politicians and positions within the Republican Party on the national stage. A similar dynamic played out on the campaign trail. McAuliffe actively wanted Trump to make an appearance alongside Youngkin, knowing that Trump had lost the state only the year before by 10 percentage points. Trump's presence could therefore mobilize voters against Youngkin. However, the Republican candidate deliberately campaigned alone, without any national Republican figures by his side. Meanwhile, McAuliffe took the opposite approach. He campaigned with former president Obama, sitting president and first lady Joe and Jill Biden, Vice President Kamala Harris, and former Georgia gubernatorial candidate Stacey Abrams.

Though McAuliffe held a small lead over Youngkin throughout the campaign, experts viewed the race as either Republican-leaning or a pure toss-up.[19] On Election Day 2021, Biden's approval rating was 8 points underwater, only 42.8 percent approving of the job he was doing as president compared to 50.8 percent disapproving.[20] As such, McAuliffe's conspicuous ties to the national Democratic Party may have ultimately contributed to his defeat, as we would generally expect in a more nationalized electoral context.

New Jersey witnessed comparably surprising results on election night, even if the incumbent still prevailed. Democratic candidate Phil Murphy first won election in 2017 by defeating his Republican challenger by nearly 18 percentage points. Given this and the strong Democratic lean of the state, experts and pundits anticipated a clear path to a Democratic hold of the office. However, by 2021 he would win by a mere 3.2 percentage points.

Polling throughout the race showed Murphy with a large lead, at times reaching double digits. Furthermore, there are about one million more registered Democrats in New Jersey than registered Republicans.[21] Murphy's campaign was generally well run, and his opponent, Jack Ciattarelli, had not previously won statewide office and was "largely unknown across the state."[22] This left many to question what went wrong. Similar to

McAuliffe in Virginia, Murphy called on some of the biggest names in the Democratic Party, such as former president Obama and Vice President Harris, to support his campaign. Meanwhile, President Biden's approval continually declined. Again, like McAuliffe, Murphy's connection to the national Democratic brand likely reduced his overall vote share.

Though Murphy managed to retain his office, those seeking legislative seats down ballot were not as fortunate. Democrats held both chambers of the state legislature for decades prior to the 2021 election. They would manage to keep that streak alive, but with smaller numbers after some shocking losses. Most notable among these losses was Senate President Stephen Sweeney. In this position, Sweeney was the second most powerful politician in the state and had served in that position longer than anyone ever had in New Jersey. For him to lose at all would have been an upset. Nonetheless, he ultimately was defeated by Edward Durr Jr., a truck driver who spent less than $10,000 on his campaign.[23] Durr received 51.7 percent of the vote compared to Sweeney's 48.3 percent. These results are consistent with recent literature demonstrating how nationalization has become pervasive enough to influence even substate-level elections (Zingher and Richman 2019; Melunsky and Richman 2020; Weinschenk et al. 2020).

Though the outcomes differed, the message from both was clear: voters had become increasingly disaffected with the Biden administration roughly a year after he defeated Trump and therefore anyone else associated with the Democratic Party (much as had been the case with the Trump administration starting in 2018). National politics were put front and center in these races, and as a result we witnessed massive swings in the partisan vote share within these states.

## SUMMARY

The 2020 elections continued a recent trend of highly nationalized elections that put President Trump front and center in the electoral arena and tied Democratic fortunes largely to former vice president Biden as the "best" shot the Democrats had to defeat the incumbent Republican at the polls. Statewide elections routinely witness candidates from the same party emerging victorious despite state-specific factors (such as COVID-19 deaths) or candidate-specific factors (such as incumbency). That nationalization continued into the off-year election cycles in 2021.

These findings have important implications for our understanding of congressional elections, democratic accountability, and legislative politics. As recently as a few decades ago, candidates' electoral fortunes were largely tied to their behavior and performance in office, and those members who were "out of step" with their district had to worry about their ability to get reelected. With the dramatic increase in nationalization, incumbents now have more to fear from getting "primaried" by a candidate more in line with ideological voters within their district as opposed to not being responsive enough to constituents who would have rewarded them for their ombudsman role in their constituencies. Theories of electoral accountability may need to be revisited, considering such high levels of nationalization. State and local conditions and individual candidate characteristics will struggle to be determinative of election outcomes if races continue to be nationalized.

Regarding legislative politics, by effectively eliminating the endorsement as a tool to curry favor with members of Congress, the president's ability to shape the legislative agenda and realize their policy goals will be diminished. If a member of Congress has their electoral fate essentially predetermined, they no longer have any incentive to cooperate on contentious issues. If the president is popular, then the member does not necessarily need an endorsement to win reelection. If the president is unpopular, the member may actively try to distance themselves from the executive to stymie the effect of national tides in their state or district. Therefore, theories of presidential-congressional relations may also need revising if the current pattern of highly nationalized politics continues.

# 9
# Conclusion

As we noted at the beginning of Chapter 2, the adage "All politics is local" seemed to accurately summarize American politics throughout most of the 20th century. Incumbent members of both parties in Congress routinely went about their business advertising themselves and their accomplishments to their constituents, funneling pork back to their congressional districts, and engaging in position-taking when that yielded marginally greater benefits than confronting the increasingly difficult issues facing our nation. During the past few decades, however, local politics has seemed to matter significantly less as politics has gradually become much more nationalized in scope, with an increasing focus on the president and national politics. In today's highly nationalized political environment, candidates running for local or statewide office are often judged by the party at the top of the ticket, as was once the case throughout most of the 19th century, when candidates from the same party had no choice but to run on the same partisan ballot.

In seeking to investigate greater nationalization in recent decades, we began this book by asking "How has nationalization influenced elections across different political eras?" After reviewing the existing literature on nationalization and analyzing 180 years of election data to better understand both the historical context and the current political climate, we offer some new insights on the ebbs and flow of nationalized politics. From this, we see that the current trend of nationalization is not new to American

*Nationalized Politics.* Jamie L. Carson, Joel Sievert, and Ryan D. Williamson, Oxford University Press.
© Oxford University Press 2024. DOI: 10.1093/oso/9780197669655.003.0009

politics. In fact, it is better characterized as a return to the norm seen throughout much of history.

In Chapter 3, we examined elections in the 19th century and more recently and found remarkable similarities across what are often perceived as very different political eras. During the 19th century, high levels of nationalization were driven largely by institutional factors such as the party ballot that was in use, which forced voters to select among candidates based on party affiliation rather than more candidate-specific factors. Following the adoption of the Australian ballot in the late 19th century, voters were given the chance to select among candidates of different parties more easily, which ultimately contributed to a less nationalized electoral environment in the ensuing decades. In time, however, nationalization once again increased, but this time it was less about institutions and more about the behavior of political elites and parties. Indeed, elections today are much more nationalized based on how political elites and candidates coordinate their electoral campaigns relative to the president and/or issues of national prominence.

In Chapter 4, we investigated the electoral connection between 1840 and 2020 and found that no level of nationalization completely inhibits the ability of candidates to cultivate a personal vote. Prior to holding all elections on the same Tuesday in November, some districts witnessed House candidates appearing at the top of the ballot instead of the president. Even though the party ballot made it extraordinarily difficult for voters to split their ticket in many races, the differential election timing mitigated nationalization in some cases throughout the 19th century. In more recent elections, we see open seats change party control more often. Therefore, there is an opportunity for candidate-specific factors like incumbency to exert an influence on election outcomes during eras of high nationalization; it is just less likely for those candidate-level characteristics to change the outcome.

We analyzed the incumbency advantage over our 180-year period in Chapter 5. There is no shortage of existing work on this phenomenon in congressional elections, especially in the modern era, but we offer a few new insights considering greater levels of nationalization in recent decades.

Even in eras of high nationalization, incumbents appear to be advantaged by their positions in office; however, the size of that advantage fluctuates depending on the level of nationalization at a given point in history. When races are more local affairs, as we saw throughout the middle part of the 20th century, the incumbency advantage is clearly much greater. That effect wanes as nationalization increases, but it does not completely go away regardless of the electoral rules or norms in place at the time.

Chapter 6 explored the relationship between nationalization and polarization in Congress. Scholars have identified many possible explanations for the recent and steady increase in the polarization of politics, but just as Hopkins (2018) suggests, we contend that nationalization can be added to that list. Indeed, we find a strong correlation between greater levels of nationalization and high polarization. This is likely a function of more moderate candidates being able to attract bipartisan support in eras of lower nationalization, which also decreases levels of polarization. Conversely, when voters base decisions more on which party they want in power instead of who is best equipped to represent their district, more ideological candidacies flourish, as we have observed over the past few decades, thereby increasing polarization in Congress.

We employed a unique survey experiment in Chapter 7 to evaluate how voters respond to the intrusion of national politics into electoral contests. We found that presidential endorsements serve as a strong cue for voters' ideological placement and favorability toward candidates. In short, voters increasingly align their views of candidates with their attitudes toward other national political actors or groups and are not necessarily evaluating candidates on their own merits. These results provide an important behavioral explanation for the rise in nationalization—namely voters' understanding of and attitudes toward politics are increasingly national in orientation, which results in the type of straight-ticket voting comparable to that of the high nationalization witnessed under the party ballot and other institutional factors throughout most of the 19th century. These findings are especially noteworthy as they help to explain the obvious similarities in nationalization across the two eras despite the distinct institutional differences.

In Chapter 8 we provided greater context for the nationalization that was observed in the 2020 elections. These races were again highly nationalized affairs, but we did see some candidate-specific effects emerge on occasion, nonetheless. However, those effects were by and large too small to change the outcome of most elections. This effect carried over into the 2021 elections and is likely to continue to do so indefinitely barring a significant change in the electoral environment, which seems quite unlikely given current political events.

## IMPLICATIONS AND FUTURE RESEARCH

Our work has timely and important implications for understanding elections in the United States. The roles of candidates and voters are fundamentally different than they were even a few short decades ago. In fact, their actions more closely mirror that of their 19th-century counterparts. Therefore, improved understanding regarding who runs, who wins, and how those winners ultimately govern may come from looking even further back in history, as much of our knowledge about electoral politics is derived from studies drawing on distinctly different eras of more localized politics. Such a perspective alters how we should think about representation, accountability, and election outcomes more broadly. Indeed, the 2022 midterm elections may stand out when compared to recent history, but they may also represent a starting point in the wholesale change in what we can expect in the future.

From our findings, new questions emerge: What would it take to reduce the level of nationalization seen in today's elections? The Progressive Era reforms ushered in profound changes and more candidate-centered politics to how elections were conducted, leading to more localized elections, but what reforms would it take to change voters' behavior in this new nationalized political environment where our electoral institutions are still candidate-centered? What are the trade-offs for candidates running in more nationalized or localized races? Lesser-known candidates may be better able to win by capitalizing on this phenomenon, but that is not likely to be a sustainable strategy over time, especially in the absence of money and other campaign resources that would be necessary for such candidates to wage an effective campaign given the advantages already accruing to incumbent legislators (even reduced as they may be compared to elections 30 or 40 years ago).

Additionally, how does nationalization influence governing and legislating? If voters become fixated on national politics and harbor increasingly negative attitudes toward the opposition, as we have seen with growing levels of negative partisanship, what incentive is there to engage in bipartisanship or expend capital on bills that have localized effects? On a related point, does nationalization impact citizens' willingness to even engage in politics? Perhaps nationalization can serve as a mobilizing effect, as suggested by the record high turnout in the 2018 and 2020 elections. Or will those years prove to be anomalies compared to future elections? What impact does increased nationalization have on citizen attitudes toward government? If national politics continues to dominate the thinking of the electorate, many may further overlook the impactful work being done at the state and local levels. Answering these and other related questions is important for understanding what the future of American politics may look like if the current patterns of nationalization continue.

## THE LIMITS OF NATIONALIZATION

The preceding chapters illustrate how the highly nationalized political climate of today has analogs in earlier political eras, even though the underlying cause of nationalization differs across each period. We know from history that greater periods of nationalization have been followed by eras of more localized politics, such as what occurred throughout the mid-20th century. In certain respects, we may already be on a path in that direction, as reflected by recent events that occurred during the 2022 election season (although it is too early as of this writing to know for certain).

One of the most notable losses in the 2022 congressional primaries was Representative Madison Cawthorn's (R-NC) defeat to Republican state senator Chuck Edwards. Cawthorn was first elected in 2020 to fill the seat previously held by President Trump's chief of staff Mark Meadows. He was one of the youngest members ever elected to the House and was seen as a rising star in the Republican Party, considering his ability to turn his personal adversity—he was partially paralyzed in a car accident in high school—into political success. During Cawthorn's first two years in office, he received substantial media attention; however, much of it was negative, ultimately alienating him from members of his party. For instance, he was stopped by police on multiple occasions for driving with a revoked license and faced multiple allegations of sexual harassment. Moreover, "he sparked backlash among colleagues, throwing around accusations about orgies and lawmakers using cocaine."[1] Despite raising large sums of money and receiving a last-minute endorsement from Trump, Cawthorn's scandal-ridden tenure in the House proved too much to overcome, and he lost to Edwards by fewer than 1,400 votes.

A week later, Trump's influence in Republican primaries was challenged yet again when former U.S. senator David Perdue failed to unseat incumbent governor Brian Kemp in Georgia. Although Kemp was endorsed by Trump when he first ran for governor in 2018, he quickly fell out of favor for his refusal to support Trump's efforts to unlawfully overturn the 2020 presidential election results in Georgia. In the months preceding the 2022 primary, Trump went all-in on Perdue and funneled over $2.5 million from his political committee into Perdue's campaign.[2] But with over one million votes cast in the Georgia Republican primary, Kemp received over 70 percent of the vote compared to less than 22 percent for Perdue. The result was a significant defeat for Trump's ability to shape political events in the election. Former Georgia lieutenant governor Geoff Duncan noted that Kemp's victory constituted a significant shift in Republican primary voters' attitudes: "At the beginning of the primary process, it felt like a Trump endorsement was the end-all, be-all for a lot of these even down-ballot candidates. But the reality is what we've gotten here today, is that voters are now returning back to their senses and realizing that leadership matters."[3]

During the fall general elections, many "election deniers" ran within the Republican ranks and openly embraced Trump's rhetoric about the 2020 election being stolen. Although a sizable number of these candidates won (mostly those representing safe districts), many others ended up losing or barely prevailed in extremely close races. Lauren Boebert (R), the incumbent in Colorado's 3rd Congressional District, is a clear example of the latter given how close her election ended up being. Boebert's Democratic opponent, former Aspen city council member Adam Frisch, campaigned as a moderate but received little support from national Democrats.[4] While most media outlets and election prognosticators expected Boebert to easily win reelection, she defeated Frisch by fewer than 600 votes.[5]

It is difficult to know whether these candidates embraced Trump's "Big Lie" as a result of the highly nationalized political era or because of his larger-than-life persona, but either way, it appears that his influence in national politics may be on the decline. Even before Trump announced that he was seeking the Republican presidential nomination in 2024, a growing number of donors and political commentators have remarked that it is time to move on from Trump in the electoral arena.[6] It also appears that Republican-aligned voters view Trump as less central to their partisan attachments. In February 2023, one poll found that 55 percent of respondents who identified as Republican voters said they considered themselves to primarily be a supporter of the Republican Party, while only 38 percent said they were primarily a supporter of Trump.[7] These findings were a significant departure from the months before the 2020 presidential election, when nearly 60 percent of Republicans said they were primarily a supporter of Trump and only 30 percent indicated that they were supporters of the Republican Party first and foremost.[8]

Although merely anecdotal, each of these examples illustrates that Trump's reach in the electoral arena has its limits. Whether these results are a sign of weakening levels of nationalization or merely a function of especially weak candidates seeking reelection (or some combination of both) is not yet clear, but it does suggest that our current highly nationalized political era may not persist indefinitely. Just as the nationalized politics of the 19th century eventually came to an end following the adoption of a series of progressive reforms, there are historical reasons to believe that we may soon be witnessing reduced levels of nationalization that have characterized politics since the 1990s. By continuing to explore both the similarities and differences in nationalization across distinct political eras, we place ourselves in a better position to evaluate events as they occur in real time.

# APPENDIX

While data from the contemporary era are readily available, obtaining data on historical elections can prove to be more of a challenge. Our data collection efforts were largely facilitated by Dubin's (1998) *United States Congressional Elections, 1788–1997*, the most comprehensive source for historical election returns. We used Dubin to identify the names and partisan affiliation of the candidates in all congressional elections before 1946, which allowed us to determine if the race included an incumbent or was an open-seat contest. We also used this source to code the vote totals for each candidate, which allows us to calculate the Democratic share of the two-party vote in each election. We relied on Martis's (1989) *The Historical Atlas of Political Parties in the United States, 1789–1989* to fill in any gaps in party identification.

There are two important issues we had to address when calculating vote shares in the historical period. First, until the Supreme Court's ruling in the 1960s, congressional districts varied considerably in terms of both population and geographic boundaries. Some states used multimember or at-large districts, which can pose possible measurement issues in terms of calculating the partisan vote share. We therefore matched the winning candidates with the losing candidates who ultimately came closest to winning, which allows for a direct comparison between vote shares in both single and multimember districts.[1] Second, although there is fluctuation in the composition of the two main parties, the Democratic Party contested elections throughout the entire period we examine. As such, we code the two-party vote with reference to the top Democratic finisher and the top opposition party finisher. For elections in the 1840s and 1850s, a Whig candidate is usually the main opposition candidate.[2] From the 1860s onward, however, the Republican Party serves as the opposition party.

Unlike data on election returns, finding information on the background of candidates from earlier time periods required far more time and effort. To extend the data on candidates' backgrounds back to 1840, we utilized a number of archives and online sources. We began our search with the *Biographical Directory of the U.S. Congress, 1774 to Present*, which provides a detailed career history of every legislator who has served in the U.S. Congress.[3] Since there was more legislative turnover throughout the 19th century (see Fiorina, Rohde, and Wissel 1975), the *Directory* allowed us to obtain background information on a large portion of the candidates from this era. For candidates who did not serve in Congress, we first turned to The Political Graveyard's website,[4] which provides background data on politicians (in addition to where they are buried). Additional background information was collected from the *New York Times* Historical Index and Google.[5]

Once we compiled background information on each candidate, we followed Jacobson's (1989) approach and measured candidate quality as whether a candidate currently holds or has previously held elective office. Although some studies advocate for more nuanced measures, we chose to utilize the simple dichotomy in our data collection for two specific reasons. First, there is considerable evidence to demonstrate that a dichotomous measure of candidate quality performs as well as more nuanced measures (Jacobson and Carson 2020). Second, our primary empirical interest is obtaining estimates of the incumbency advantage over a broader timespan. As such, it is important to keep our coding scheme the same as the original studies, which utilize, or are extensions of, this dichotomous measure.

# NOTES

## CHAPTER 1

1. Carl M. Cannon, "Democrats in a Dilemma: Run with or from Clinton?," *Baltimore Sun*, October 9, 1994, https://www.baltimoresun.com/news/bs-xpm-1994-10-09-1994282050-story.html.
2. Richard L. Berke, "Party Chairman Attacks 4 Democrats Who Failed," *New York Times*, May 26, 1994, https://www.nytimes.com/1994/05/26/us/party-chairman-attacks-4-democrats-who-failed.html.
3. Thomas B. Edsall, "GOP Gains House Seat Hatcher Held," *Washington Post*, May 25, 1994, https://www.washingtonpost.com/archive/politics/1994/05/25/gop-gains-house-seat-natcher-held/d0a663be-e941-4817-9352-8c8f61c033ee/.
4. Henry Enton, "There Were No Purple States on Tuesday," *FiveThirtyEight*, November 10, 2016, https://fivethirtyeight.com/features/there-were-no-purple-states-on-tuesday/.
5. Geoffrey Skelley, "Split-Ticket Voting Hit a New Low In 2018 Senate and Governor Races," *FiveThirtyEight*, November 19, 2018, https://fivethirtyeight.com/features/split-ticket-voting-hit-a-new-low-in-2018-senate-and-governor-races/.
6. As of the 2020 election, only six states allow a straight-ticket voting option: Alabama, Indiana, Michigan, Kentucky, Oklahoma, and South Carolina. On this point, see https://www.ncsl.org/research/elections-and-campaigns/straight-ticket-voting.aspx.
7. Fred Schulte, "States Continue War over Obamacare," Center for Public Integrity, January 21, 2015, https://publicintegrity.org/health/states-continue-war-over-obamacare/.
8. To be clear, we view nationalization as a fundamentally different concept from national political tides or conditions. Whereas nationalization suggests the influence of national factors on specific races, the latter concept often reflects specific factors such as changing economic or political circumstances that directly influence presidential or congressional election results in a given year.
9. *Roll Call* Staff, "Here Are the 15 Democrats Who Didn't Vote for Pelosi as Speaker," *Roll Call*, January 3, 2019, https://www.rollcall.com/2019/01/03/here-are-the-15-democrats-who-didnt-vote-for-pelosi-as-speaker/.

10. Kate Ackley, "Blue Wave Survivors: After Narrow 2018 Victory, Will GOP's Rodney Davis Keep His Seat This Year?," *Roll Call*, October 12, 2020, https://rollcall.com/2020/10/12/blue-wave-survivors-after-narrow-2018-victory-will-gops-rodney-davis-keep-his-seat-this-year/.

## CHAPTER 2

1. Andrew Gelman, "All Politics Is Local? The Debate and the Graphs," *FiveThirtyEight*, January 3, 2011, https://fivethirtyeight.com/features/all-politics-is-local-the-debate-and-the-graphs/.
2. Paul Kane, "All Politics Is Local? In the Era of Trump, Not Anymore," *Washington Post*, February 25, 2017, https://www.washingtonpost.com/powerpost/all-politics-is-local-in-the-era-of-trump-not anymore/2017/02/25/9a15bc94-fab2-11e6-9845-576c69081518_story.html.
3. Elaina Plott, "In a Small Alabama Town, Suddenly All Politics Is National," *New York Times*, October 11, 2020, https://www.nytimes.com/2020/10/11/us/politics/in-a-small-alabama-town-suddenly-all-politics-is-national.html.
4. The term "nationalization" has also been used to describe the nature of the party system in a given country (see, e.g., Chhibber and Kollman 2004; Morgenstern, Swindle, and Castagnola 2009). Given the relative stability of the party system in the United States, this conceptualization of nationalization is less relevant to our study.
5. See Chapter 3 for a more detailed discussion of the alternative measurement strategies for nationalization.
6. Bullock and Owen (2021) devote a substantial amount of attention to the special election that occurred in 2017 in Georgia's Sixth District, where Republican Karen Handel narrowly defeated Democrat Jon Ossoff. In total, about $55 million was spent on the special election, much of it from out-of-state spending, due to the enormous national attention on the race.
7. Don Gonyea, "Trump Yanks Endorsement of Alabama Senate Candidate Brooks, Who Said to Get Past 2020," NPR, March 23, 2022, https://www.npr.org/2022/03/23/1088264503/donald-trump-mo-brooks-withdraws-alabama-endorsement.
8. Natalie Allison, "Trump Endorses Britt in Alabama Republican Senate Race," *Politico*, June 10, 2022, https://www.politico.com/news/2022/06/10/trump-endorses-britt-in-alabama-republican-senate-race-00038991.
9. Jonathan Swan and Lachlan Markey, "J. D. Vance's Trump-Like Effect," *Axios*, May 4, 2022, https://www.axios.com/2022/05/04/jd-vance-trump-ohio-senate?utm_source=twitter&utm_medium=social&utm_campaign=editorial&utm_content=politics-jdvance; Shane Goldmacher and Maggie Haberman, "Tucker, Thiel and Trump: How J. D. Vance Won in Ohio," *New York Times*, May 4, 2022, https://www.nytimes.com/2022/05/04/us/politics/jd-vance-trump-ohio-fox-news.html.
10. Anthony Zurcher, "J. D. Vance: Trump-Backed Contender Clinches Ohio Senate Race," BBC News, May 4, 2022, https://www.bbc.com/news/world-us-canada-61315649.

11. Julia Mueller and Hannah Schoenbaum, "Rig the System: GOP Candidates for Secretary of State Run on Trump's Election Denial Platform," *USA Today*, June 27, 2022, https://www.usatoday.com/story/news/politics/elections/2022/06/27/trump-election-fraud-secretary-state-campaigns/7748150001/?gnt-cfr=1.
12. Josh Robin and Rachel Tillman, "A 'Dangerous Position' for Democracy: Election Deniers Bring Trump's Fraud Claims to Secretary of State Races," *NY1*, August 9, 2022, https://www.ny1.com/nyc/all-boroughs/news/2022/08/08/secretary-of-state-races-election-donald-trump-fraud-claims-arizona-nevada-michigan.

## CHAPTER 3

1. The 1874 midterm elections were spread out from June 1, 1874, to September 7, 1875, with Oregon going first and California holding their elections last (Dubin 1998). Prior to the early 1880s, congressional elections in states were often held months before or after the traditional November date for elections.
2. The greater variability during historical presidential elections is likely a function of election timing since congressional elections were held in the months before and after the presidential election year throughout the 19th century (Carson and Sievert 2017; Engstrom and Kernell 2005).
3. One notable exception was the period 1948 through 1956, when the correlation coefficient was over 0.80.
4. See Chapter 5 for a more detailed discussion of the Gelman and King estimator.

## CHAPTER 4

1. The three instances in which the president's party gained seats are the 1934, 1998, and 2002 elections. There was a fourth instance, the 1902 midterms, when the president's party gained seats, but these gains were primarily due to the House chamber expanding from 357 to 386 members. In fact, the Republican majority saw its overall seat share drop between the 57th Congress (1901–1903) and the 58th Congress (1903–1905).
2. Jake Sherman and Anna Palmer, "Behind Pence's Plan to Rescue the Republican Majority in 2018," *Politico*, February 1, 2018, https://www.politico.com/story/2018/02/01/mike-pence-republicans-congress-midterms-381261.
3. For additional evidence of an electoral connection outside of the modern era, see also Finocchiaro and Jenkins (2016), Finocchiaro and McKenzie (2018), and Swift (1987).
4. In presidential election years, we define "president's party" based on which party won control of the White House that year. For midterms, partisanship is coded with reference to the current occupant of the White House. Except for 1866, partisan control of the White House does not change between presidential and midterm elections.
5. See Gary Jacobson's (2007, 2015a, 2015c, 2019a, 2021) various election-specific analyses.

## CHAPTER 5

1. In total, there were only 23 Republican-held districts where former secretary of state Hillary Clinton won the most votes in 2016 and 12 Democratic districts where President Donald Trump received more votes. By comparison, the 2000 election, another year when the Democratic candidate won the popular vote and lost the Electoral College, produced 40 Republican-held districts that voted for Vice President Al Gore and 46 Democratic districts in which President George W. Bush received more votes.
2. Jamie Lovegrove, "Democrats Prep to Target Dallas Rep. Pete Sessions in 2018," *Dallas Morning News*, February 2, 2017, https://www.dallasnews.com/news/politics/2017/02/02/democrats-prep-to-target-dallas-rep-pete-sessions-in-2018/.
3. Griffin Connolly, "Trump Jr., Top Trump PAC Helping Vulnerable GOP Rep. Pete Sessions," *Roll Call*, October 10, 2018, https://rollcall.com/2018/10/10/trump-jr-top-trump-pac-helping-vulnerable-gop-rep-pete-sessions/.
4. Gromer Jeffers Jr., "Health Care, Pelosi, Trump: Pete Sessions–Colin Allred Showdown Mirrors National Struggle for House," *Dallas Morning News*, November 2, 2018, https://www.dallasnews.com/news/2018/11/01/health-care-pelosi-trump-pete-sessions-colin-allred-showdown-mirrors-national-struggle-for-house/.
5. Critics of congressional redistricting as a possible explanation for the incumbency advantage quickly pointed out that since incumbent senators were also reelected at very high rates, redistricting could not be a contributing factor given that state boundaries do not change every 10 years. On this point, see Tufte (1973).
6. See also Jacobson (1987) for a discussion suggesting that incumbents are no safer than they had been in the past. For a critique of this argument, see Bauer and Hibbing (1989) and Ansolabehere, Brady, and Fiorina (1992).
7. For example, in 2016, there were 23 congressional districts in which Hillary Clinton won the popular vote but a Republican incumbent won reelection. In total, a quality challenger emerged in only 6 of these 23 districts.
8. Although Erikson (1971) noted that traditional measures of the incumbency advantage, such as the retirement slump and the sophomore surge, could result in biased estimates, Gelman and King (1990) were the first to formally demonstrate the nature of this bias.
9. See the Appendix for a more detailed discussion about collection of the historical congressional elections data.
10. The key theoretical and empirical assumption in this case is that in close elections, candidates on either side of the electoral threshold will not be systematically different, save for their treatment status (Lee 2008). Hainmueller, Hall, and Snyder (2015, 707) note that the estimates obtained through a RDD are "local" in the sense that it "only estimates incumbency advantages for extremely close elections—technically, in fact, it only provides an estimate for hypothetical districts with exactly tied elections."
11. Since these estimators require the comparison of stable districts, we exclude the first election immediately following the decennial reapportionment. We also exclude districts that were redrawn middecade.

12. Jacobson (2015b) offers a modified Gelman-King measure that uses presidential vote instead of lagged Democratic vote share. Unfortunately, this approach is more difficult to employ for historical elections because we do not have presidential vote data for nearly as many districts. Our substantive conclusions about the changes in the incumbency advantage over time remain unchanged if we employ the modified Gelman-King measure.
13. Erikson and Titiunik (2015, 113) contend that strategic retirement is not an issue for their proposed estimation process because "in the period we study, only one open seat winner within the 48–52% vote window retired at election $t+1$." The same cannot be said for earlier historical elections when a greater number of open-seat winners did not seek a second term. To examine whether this was due to strategic retirement, we analyzed the average margin of victory for open-seat winners who did and did not seek a second term in office. We found no substantively meaningful differences between these groups throughout the 19th century. Indeed, the only substantive differences were found in more recent decades, but there was not a consistent pattern to the estimated differences.
14. Although scholars often utilize various definitions of a close election, we stick with the more conventional definition of a race in which the winner won by less than 5 percentage points.
15. For the analysis reported in this chapter we use a local linear specification (see Eggers et al. 2015), but our substantive findings are the same if we use a higher-order polynomial specification.
16. It is important to note that the nationalization of elections is a distinct concept from national conditions, such as the state of the economy or presidential popularity, which can favorably influence strategic candidate entry decisions (Jacobson 1989).
17. We focus on elections from 1840 to 1870 for two reasons. First, Carson and Roberts (2013) provide a systematic analysis of the incumbency advantage from 1872 to 1944. We therefore focus on the earlier periods not covered by their analysis. Second, Congress passed legislation in 1872 to prohibit the use of off-November congressional elections. Although some states continued to elect their members of Congress outside of November after this point (Engstrom 2012, 375–376), the number of post-November elections decreases substantially after 1872, and we do not have enough cases to conduct the analysis. Our substantive conclusions are the same if we extend the analysis to the 1880s.
18. We define "marginal districts" as those in which the Democratic presidential vote was greater than 45 percent and less than 55 percent.
19. During the party ballot era, there were still instances in which congressional candidates may have been impacted by gubernatorial coattails. Carson and Sievert (2018) explore this possibility for midterm election years in the 1840s through the 1880s. Their findings reveal two important patterns. First, many midterm congressional elections were not held at the same time as gubernatorial contests. Second, their analysis suggests that candidate recruitment had a larger impact on which party won than the presence of a gubernatorial candidate. These results appear to comport with our claim about the relative impact of national and local forces across midterm and presidential elections. Furthermore, it is important to note

that the nationalization of statewide elections, both historically and in the modern era, exhibits a pattern over time similar to those reported in Figure 5.1 and varies based on both electoral institutions and election timing (Engstrom and Kernell 2014; Sievert and McKee 2019).
20. Such an interpretation is consistent with Ansolabehere, Snyder, and Stewart's (2001) findings regarding candidate positioning in House elections.
21. While it is beyond the scope of this book, we would note that scholars pointing to changes in the media environment that place greater emphasis on national than on local issues may help contribute to the overall nationalization of politics (Hopkins 2018). Similarly, scholars may want to consider how the proliferation of spending by political action committees following the Supreme Court's *Citizens United* decision impacts that variability of the incumbency advantage and related phenomena.

CHAPTER 6

1. Jonathan Martin, "Eric Cantor Defeated by David Brat, Tea Party Challenger, in G.O.P. Primary Upset," *New York Times*, June 10, 2014, https://www.nytimes.com/2014/06/11/us/politics/eric-cantor-loses-gop-primary.html; Mark Z. Barabak, "The Earthquake That Toppled Eric Cantor: How Did It Happen?," *Los Angeles Times*, June 11, 2014, https://www.latimes.com/nation/politics/politicsnow/la-pn-earthquake-toppled-cantor-20140611-story.html.
2. In seeking to explain the corresponding growth in polarization within the Senate (where the same procedural tools do not exist), Theriault (2013) claims that replacement by former House members who were already polarized accounts for much of the increased polarization in the upper chamber. See Lee (2009), however, for an alternative argument about procedural partisanship in the Senate.
3. Although there are several explanations for the lack of competition, we can profitably categorize these findings as pinpointing one of the following influences: money (see, e.g., Abramowitz, Alexander, and Gunning 2006; Gimpel, Lee, Pearson-Merkowitz 2008; Green and Krasno 1988; Jacobson 1978), the role of challengers (e.g., Carson 2005; Jacobson 1987; Mayhew 1974a), and polarization (Canes-Wrone, Brady, and Cogan 2002; Carson et al. 2010; Levendusky 2009; McCarty, Poole, and Rosenthal 2016).
4. Jacobson's (2015c) claim about the Republicans' structural advantage in House elections argues against Bonica and Cox's (2018) contention that competition for the House majority has increased in recent decades.
5. Despite this, these averages hide some sizable swings. For instance, the number of split districts was 15.8 percent in the 1872 presidential election but more than doubled to 34.8 percent during the 1874 midterms.
6. For more evidence of this specific point, see Ansolabehere, Snyder, and Stewart (2001).
7. One additional benefit to including these fixed effects is that it accounts for any differences in the distribution of the presidential vote measure across time and constituencies.

8. We define "a decade" as the period within the decennial reapportionment cycle. For example, the 1990s includes all elections from 1992, the first after the reapportionment, to 2000.

## CHAPTER 7

1. Jack Brewster, "Poll: 56% of Biden Voters Say They're Voting for Him Because He's 'Not Trump,'" *Forbes*, August 13, 2020, https://www.forbes.com/sites/jackbrewster/2020/08/13/poll-56-of-biden-voters-say-theyre-voting-for-him-because-hes-not-trump/?sh=32df81ad6132.
2. The 2016 feeling thermometer data have not yet been included in the ANES Timeseries file due to ongoing data correction. Please see the Timeseries file codebook for details.
3. Quint Forgey, "'Kevin Is in Very Good Shape': House Republican Shrugs off McCarthy Audio Controversy," *Politico*, April 24, 2022, https://www.politico.com/news/2022/04/24/mccaul-mccarthy-audio-controversy-trump-00027372.
4. Our survey experiment took place during the primaries for the 2022 congressional midterms, which was fortuitous for our purposes since both the sitting Democratic president, Biden, and former Republican president, Trump, actively endorsed candidates. While Trump was the more active endorser during this period, the important takeaway is that our survey was in the field at a time when it was reasonable to expect that both presidents would be actively endorsing a potential candidate.
5. Respondents were also able to indicate that they were "not sure" about a candidate's qualifications for office. We omit these responses from our analysis.
6. Domenico Montanaro, "Biden Approval Hits Another New Low as More Democrats Sour on Him, Poll Finds," National Public Radio, July 20, 2022, https://www.npr.org/2022/07/20/1112297499/biden-approval-hits-another-new-low-as-more-democrats-sour-on-him-poll-finds.

## CHAPTER 8

1. Stephanie McCrummen, Beth Reinhard, and Alice Crites, "Woman Says Roy Moore Initiated Sexual Encounter When She Was 14, He Was 32," *Washington Post*, November 9, 2017, https://www.washingtonpost.com/investigations/woman-says-roy-moore-initiated-sexual-encounter-when-she-was-14-he-was-32/2017/11/09/1f495878-c293-11e7-afe9-4f60b5a6c4a0_story.html.
2. John Sharp, "Was Richard Shelby's Call for a Write-in Vote a 'Very Big Factor' in Roy Moore's Defeat?," *AL.com*, December 13, 2017, https://www.al.com/news/mobile/2017/12/was_richard_shelbys_call_for_a.html.
3. Mary Bowerman, "Twitter Thanks #BlackWomen for Voting for Democrat Doug Jones in Alabama Senate Election," *USA Today*, December 13, 2017, https://www.usatoday.com/story/news/politics/onpolitics/2017/12/13/twitter-thanks-blackwomen-voting-democrat-doug-jones-alabama-senate-election/947403001/.

4. Sean Sullivan and David Weigel, "One Wide-Open Question about Doug Jones: What Kind of Senator Will He Be?," *Washington Post*, December 13, 2017, https://www.washingtonpost.com/powerpost/one-wide-open-question-about-doug-jones-what-kind-of-senator-will-he-be/2017/12/13/e3c1068e-e010-11e7-8679-a9728984779c_story.html.
5. Seth McLaughlin, "Doug Jones Represents Conservative Alabama, Votes Like New England Liberal," *AP News*, October 17, 2018, https://apnews.com/article/bbd2696b0d44076ce8bb01181588b500.
6. Adam Edelman and Rebecca Shabad, "Alabama Democrat Doug Jones Walks Tightrope with Trump and His Own Party," *NBC News*, July 2, 2018, https://www.nbcnews.com/politics/congress/alabama-democrat-doug-jones-walks-tightrope-trump-his-own-party-n887501.
7. Glenn Stephens, "Jones Starts Last Leg of Campaign with Almost 16 Times as Much Money as Tuberville," *Birmingham Watch*, July 15, 2020, https://birminghamwatch.org/jones-starts-last-leg-campaign-almost-16-times-much-money-tuberville/.
8. Mike Cason, "Tuberville Says 'God Sent Us Donald Trump' in New Radio Ad," *AL.com*, February 18, 2020, https://www.al.com/news/2020/01/tuberville-says-god-sent-us-donald-trump-in-new-radio-ad.html.
9. Mike Cason, "Straight-Party Voters Could Doom Doug Jones in US Senate Race against Tommy Tuberville," *AL.com*, October 30, 2020, https://www.al.com/news/2020/10/straight-party-voters-could-doom-doug-jones-in-us-senate-race-against-tommy-tuberville.html.
10. Brian Lyman, "Tuberville Pitches to Base, Doug Jones Attempts Coalition," *Montgomery Advertiser*, October 28, 2020, https://www.montgomeryadvertiser.com/story/news/2020/10/28/alabama-senate-tommy-tuberville-pitches-base-doug-jones-attempts-coalition/3719427001/.
11. These figures include the two special elections in Georgia. For Arkansas, which did not feature a Democratic candidate, this figure includes the vote share won by the Libertarian candidate. For Louisiana, which utilizes a jungle primary with multiple candidates, the vote shares are calculated for all Democratic candidates versus all Republican candidates.
12. Ellen Barry, "The Democrats Went All Out against Susan Collins, Rural Maine Grimaced," *New York Times*, November 17, 2020, https://www.nytimes.com/2020/11/17/us/maine-susan-collins.html.
13. Rachel Bade and Erica Werner, "Centrist House Democrats Lash Out at Liberal Colleagues, Blame Far-Left Views for Costing the Party Seats," *Washington Post*, November 5, 2020, https://www.washingtonpost.com/politics/house-democrats-pelosi-election/2020/11/05/1ddae5ca-1f6e-11eb-90dd-abd0f7086a91_story.html.
14. Meagan Flynn, "Spanberger Sparked a Debate about 'Defund the Police' Attacks. Cameron Webb Slogged through Them," *Washington Post*, November 11, 2020, https://www.washingtonpost.com/local/virginia-politics/webb-spanberger-defund-attacks/2020/11/11/9afd6408-2426-11eb-952e-0c475972cfc0_story.html.
15. These ratings were taken from the last rating offered on October 29, 2020. They have been collapsed from a 7-point scale to a 3-point scale for ease of presentation and interpretation.

16. Daniel Wood and Geoff Brumfiel, "Pro-Trump Counties Now Have Far Higher COVID Death Rates. Misinformation Is to Blame," NPR, December 5, 2021, https://www.npr.org/sections/health-shots/2021/12/05/1059828993/data-vaccine-misinformation-trump-counties-covid-death-rate.
17. "Forecasting the US Elections," *The Economist*, November 3, 2020, https://projects.economist.com/us-2020-forecast/house.
18. Quinn Scanlan, "McAuliffe, Youngkin Spar over Vision for Commonwealth in 1st Va. Gubernatorial Debate," *ABC News*, September 17, 2021, https://abcnews.go.com/Politics/mcauliffe-youngkin-spar-vision-commonwealth-1st-va-gubernatorial/story?id=80057575.
19. Gregory S. Schneider, Laura Vozzella, Karina Elwood, Scott Clement, and Emily Guskin, "Virginia Governor's Race a Toss-up as Election Day Nears, Post-Schar School Poll Finds," *Washington Post*, October 29, 2021, https://www.washingtonpost.com/dc-md-va/2021/10/29/virginia-governors-race-poll/
20. "How Popular Is Joe Biden?," *FiveThirtyEight*, https://projects.fivethirtyeight.com/biden-approval-rating/. Accessed August 30, 2022.
21. *NJ Globe* Staff, "N.J. Still Has 1 Million More Democrats Than Republicans, but August Gave GOP an 8-1 Registration Edge," *New Jersey Globe*, September 7, 2021, https://newjerseyglobe.com/campaigns/n-j-still-has-1-million-more-democrats-than-republicans-but-august-gave-gop-an-8-1-registration-edge/.
22. Nancy Solomon and Ruth Talbot, "Democrat Phil Murphy Is Reelected in an Extremely Tight Race for New Jersey Governor," NPR, November 3, 2021, https://www.npr.org/2021/11/02/1050183040/new-jersey-governor-election-results-murphy-ciattarelli.
23. Felicia Sonmez, "Edward Durr Jr., Republican Truck Driver and Political Novice, Defeats Longtime New Jersey State Senate President Steve Sweeney," *Washington Post*, November 5, 2021, https://www.washingtonpost.com/politics/durr-defeats-sweeney/2021/11/04/3c2b9f52-3d85-11ec-bfad-8283439871ec_story.html.

## CHAPTER 9

1. Myah Ward, "Cawthorn Loses Primary in North Carolina: The Controversial Republican Was Defeated by State Senator Chuck Edwards," *Politico*, May 17, 2022, https://www.politico.com/news/2022/05/17/cawthorn-north-carolina-primary-00033315?utm_source=facebook&utm_medium=news_tab.
2. Daniel Klaidman and Michael Isikoff, "Georgia Gov. Kemp Defeats Trump-Backed Challenger, Former Senator Perdue in GOP Primary," *Yahoo!News*, May 24, 2022, https://www.yahoo.com/news/georgia-gov-kemp-defeats-trump-backed-challenger-former-sen-perdue-in-gop-primary-004712220.html.
3. Riley Bunch, "Kemp Stomps Trump-Backed David Perdue in Georgia Governor Primary," Georgia Public Broadcasting, May 24, 2022, https://www.gpb.org/news/2022/05/24/kemp-stomps-trump-backed-david-perdue-in-georgia-governor-primary.
4. Jesse Paul, "Lauren Boebert Narrowly Wins Reelection in Colorado's 3rd Congressional District after Adam Frisch Concedes," *Colorado Sun*, November 18,

2022, https://coloradosun.com/2022/11/18/lauren-boebert-adam-frisch-final-resu lts-colorado/.
5. "2022 House Forecast: Consensus Forecast," *270toWin*, November 7, 2022, https:// www.270towin.com/2022-house-election/consensus-2022-house-forecast.
6. Julia Mueller, "GOP Mega-Donor Says 'It's Time to Move On' from Trump," *The Hill*, November 6, 2022, https://thehill.com/homenews/campaign/3722409-gop-megadonor-says-its-time-to-move-on-from-trump/; Amanda L. Gordon and Magan Crane, "GOP Donors Worth $85 Billion Say It's Time to Move On from Trump," *Bloomberg*, November 16, 2022, https://www.bloomberg.com/news/articles/2022-11-16/schwarzman-turns-back-on-trump-calls-for-new-generation?leadSource=uverify%20wall; David Freedlander, "The GOP Is Starting to Plot against Donald Trump," *Politico*, February 9, 2023, https://www.politico.com/news/magazine/2023/02/09/gop-trump-2024-election-00081944.
7. Echelon Insights, February 2023 Voter Verified Omnibus, https://echeloninsights.com/in-the-news/feb-2024-past-presidents-approval/.
8. Echelon Insights, February 2021 Voter Verified Omnibus, https://echeloninsights.com/in-the-news/february-omnibus-political-update/.

## APPENDIX

1. An alternative method for dealing with this issue would be to employ Niemi, Jackman, and Winsky's (1991) approach to calculating vote share in multimember districts by generating sets of pseudo-pairs between winning and losing candidates. Unfortunately, this approach can lead to an artificial inflation in candidate vote share among nonsymmetrically contested races where candidates appear to receive 100 percent of the vote.
2. In the 1850s, elections in the southern states typically featured a Democrat and an American Party candidate. Most studies treat the American Party as a third party, but in the South it can be effectively thought of as one of the two major parties in congressional elections. As such, we treat the American Party as the second party in these states when calculating the two-party vote.
3. The biographical directory link is http://bioguide.congress.gov/biosearch/biosearch.asp.
4. The Political Graveyard website can be accessed at http://www.politicalgraveyard.com.
5. We were able to collect background data on just over 75 percent of the candidates in elections before 1944. In cases where we could not find any background information, we followed Jacobson's (1989) approach and coded these candidates as nonquality. The results we report are robust to alternative specifications, such as Carson and Roberts's (2013) imputation strategy.

# REFERENCES

Abramowitz, Alan I. 1985. "Economic Conditions, Presidential Popularity, and Voting Behavior in Midterm Congressional Elections." *Journal of Politics* 47 (1): 31–43.
Abramowitz, Alan I. 1989. "Campaign Spending in U.S. Senate Elections." *Legislative Studies Quarterly* 14: 487–507.
Abramowitz, Alan I. 1991. "Incumbency, Campaign Spending, and the Decline of Competition in U.S. House Elections." *Journal of Politics* 53: 34–56.
Abramowitz, Alan I. 2010. *The Disappearing Center: Engaged Citizens, Polarization, and American Democracy*. New Haven, CT: Yale University Press.
Abramowitz, Alan I., Brad Alexander, and Matthew Gunning. 2006. "Incumbency, Redistricting, and the Decline of Competition in House Elections." *Journal of Politics* 68 (1): 75–88.
Abramowitz, Alan I., and Steven Webster. 2016. "The Rise of Negative Partisanship and the Nationalization of U.S. Elections in the 21st Century." *Electoral Studies* 41: 12–22.
Adams, James, Samuel Merrill III, Elizabeth N. Simas, and Walter J. Stone. 2011. "When Candidates Value Good Character: A Spatial Model with Applications to Congressional Elections." *Journal of Politics* 73 (1): 17–30.
Ahler, Douglas J., and Gaurav Sood. 2018. "The Parties In Our Heads: Misperceptions about Party Composition and Their Consequences." *Journal of Politics* 80 (3): 964–981.
Aldrich, John. 2010. *Why Parties? A Second Look*. Chicago: University of Chicago Press.
Aldrich, John H., Jamie L. Carson, Brad T. Gomez, and Jennifer L. Merolla. 2022. *Change and Continuity in the 2020 Elections*. Lanham, MD: Rowman & Littlefield.
Alford, John R., and John H. Hibbing. 1981. "Increased Incumbency Advantage in the House." *Journal of Politics* 43: 1042–1061.
Algara, Carlos, and Isaac Hale. 2019. "The Distortionary Effects of Racial Animus on Proximity Voting in the 2016 Elections." *Electoral Studies* 58 (1): 58–69.
Algara, Carlos, and Isaac Hale. 2020. "White Racial Attitudes and Political Cross-Pressures in Nationalized Elections: The Case of the Republican Coalition in the Trump Era." *Electoral Studies* 68 (1): 1–13.
Amira, Karyn. 2022. "Donald Trump's Effect on Who Is Considered 'Conservative.'" *American Politics Research* 50 (5): 682–693.

Amlani, Sharif, and Carlos Algara. 2021. "Partisanship and Nationalization in American Elections: Evidence from Presidential, Senatorial, and Gubernatorial Elections in US Counties, 1872–2020." *Electoral Studies* 73: 102387.

Ang, Adrian U-Jin, and L. Marvin Overby. 2008. "Retirements, Retentions, and the Balance of Partisan Power in Contemporary Congressional Politics." *Journal of Legislative Studies* 14 (3): 339–352.

Ansolabehere, Stephen, David Brady, and Morris Fiorina. 1992. "The Vanishing Marginals and Electoral Responsiveness." *British Journal of Political Science* 22: 21–38.

Ansolabehere, Stephen, James M. Snyder Jr., and Charles Stewart III. 2000. "Old Voters, New Voters, and the Personal Vote: Using Redistricting to Measure the Incumbency Advantage." *American Journal of Political Science* 44: 17–34.

Ansolabehere, Steven, James Snyder, and Charles Stewart III. 2001. "Candidate Positioning in U.S. House Elections." *American Journal of Political Science* 45 (1): 136–159.

Arcenaux, Kevin, and Robin Kolodny. 2009. "Educating the Least Informed: Group Endorsements in a Grass Roots Campaign." *American Journal of Political Science* 53 (4): 755–770.

Arnold, R. Douglas. 1990. *The Logic of Congressional Action*. New Haven, CT: Yale University Press.

Atkeson, Lonna Rae, and Randall W. Partin. 1995. "Economic Referendum Voting: A Comparison of Gubernatorial and Senatorial Elections." *American Political Science Review* 89 (1): 99–107.

Bafumi, Joseph, and Michael C. Herron. 2010. "Leapfrog Representation and Extremism: A Study of American Voters and Their Members of Congress." *American Political Science Review* 104 (3): 519–542.

Ballard, Andrew O., Hans J. G. Hassell, and Michael Heseltine. 2021. "Be Careful What You Wish For: The Impacts of President Trump's Midterm Endorsements." *Legislative Studies Quarterly* 46 (2): 459–491.

Banda, Kevin K. 2016. "Issue Ownership, Issue Positions, and Candidate Assessment." *Political Communication* 33 (4): 651–666.

Banda, Kevin K. 2021. "Issue Ownership Cues and Candidate Support." *Party Politics* 27 (3): 552–564.

Bankert, Alexa. 2020. "Negative and Positive Partisanship in the 2016 U.S. Presidential Elections." *Political Behavior* 43: 1467–1485.

Barber, Michael, and Jeremy C. Pope. 2019. "Does Party Trump Ideology? Disentangling Party and Ideology in America." *American Political Science Review* 113 (1): 38–54.

Bartels, Larry M. 1998. "Electoral Continuity and Change, 1868–1996." *Electoral Studies* 17 (3): 301–326.

Bartels, Larry M. 2000. "Partisanship and Voting Behavior, 1952–1996." *American Journal of Political Science* 44 (1): 35–50.

Bauer, Monica, and John R. Hibbing. 1989. "Which Incumbents Lose in House Elections: A Response to Jacobson's 'The Marginals Never Vanished.'" *American Journal of Political Science* 33 (February): 262–271.

Benedictis-Kessner, Justin de, and Christopher Warshaw. 2020. "Accountability for the Local Economy at All Levels of Government in United States Elections." *American Political Science Review* 114 (3): 660–676.

# References

Bensel, Richard F. 2004. *The American Ballot Box in the Mid-Nineteenth Century*. New York: Cambridge University Press.

Bianco, William T., David B. Spence, and John D. Wilkerson. 1996. "The Electoral Connection in the Early Congress: The Case of the Compensation Act of 1816." *American Journal of Political Science* 40: 145–171.

Bonica, Adam. 2014. "Mapping the Ideological Marketplace." *American Journal of Political Science* 58 (2): 367–387.

Bonica, Adam, and Gary Cox. 2018. "Ideological Extremists in the U.S. Congress: Out of Step but Still in Office." *Quarterly Journal of Political Science* 13 (2): 207–236.

Born, Richard. 1979. "Generational Replacement and the Growth of Incumbent Reelection Margins in the U.S. House." *American Political Science Review* 73: 811–817.

Born, Richard. 2008. "Party Polarization and the Rise of Partisan Voting in U.S. House Elections." *American Politics Research* 36 (1): 62–84.

Box-Steffensmeier, Janet. 1996. "A Dynamic Analysis of the Role of War Chests in Campaign Strategy." *American Journal of Political Science* 40: 352–371.

Brace, Paul. 1985. "A Probabilistic Approach to Retirement from the U.S. Congress." *Legislative Studies Quarterly* 10 (1): 107–123.

Brady, David W., Robert D'Onofrio, and Morris P. Fiorina. 2000. "The Nationalization of Electoral Forces Revisited." In *Continuity and Change in House Elections*, eds. David W. Brady, John F. Cogan, and Morris P. Fiorina, 130–148. Palo Alto, CA: Stanford University Press.

Brasher, Holly. 2009. "The Dynamic Character of Political Party Evaluations." *Party Politics* 15 (1): 69–92.

Brown, Adam R. 2010. "Are Governors Responsible for the State Economy? Partisanship, Blame, and Divided Federalism." *Journal of Politics* 72 (3): 605–615.

Bullock, Charles S., III, and Karen L. Owen. 2021. *Special Elections: The Backdoor Entrance to Congress*. New York: Oxford University Press.

Burden, Barry C., and David C. Kimball. 2004. *Why Americans Split Their Tickets: Campaign, Competition, and Divided Government*. Ann Arbor: University of Michigan Press.

Burnham, Walter Dean. 1965. "The Changing Sphere of the American Political Universe." *American Political Science Review* 59 (1): 7–28.

Buttice, Matthew K., and Walter J. Stone. 2012. "Candidates Matter: Policy and Quality Differences in Congressional Elections." *Journal of Politics* 74 (3): 870–887.

Cain, Bruce, John Ferejohn, and Morris P. Fiorina. 1987. *The Personal Vote*. Cambridge, MA: Harvard University Press.

Campbell, Angus, Philip E. Converse, Warren E. Miller, and Donald E. Stokes. 1960. *The American Voter*. Chicago: University of Chicago Press.

Campbell, James E. 1985. "Explaining Presidential Losses in Midterm Elections." *Journal of Politics* 47 (4): 11401157.

Campbell, James E. 1997. "The Presidential Pulse and the 1994 Midterm Congressional Election." *Journal of Politics* 59 (3): 830–857.

Canes-Wrone, Brandice, David W. Brady, and John F. Cogan. 2002. "Out of Step Out of Office: Electoral Accountability and House Members' Voting." *American Political Science Review* 96 (1): 127–140.

Carsey, Thomas M., and Geoffrey C. Layman. 2006. "Changing Sides or Changing Minds? Party Identification and Policy Preferences in the American Electorate." *American Journal of Political Science* 50 (2): 464–477.

Carsey, Thomas M., and Gerald C. Wright. 1998. "State and National Factors in Gubernatorial and Senatorial Elections: A Rejoinder." *American Journal of Political Science* 42 (3): 1008–1011.

Carson, Jamie L. 2005. "Strategy, Selection, and Candidate Competition in U.S. House and Senate Elections." *Journal of Politics* 67 (1): 1–28.

Carson, Jamie L., and Erik J. Engstrom. 2005. "Assessing the Electoral Connection: Evidence from the Early United States." *American Journal of Political Science* 49 (4): 746–757.

Carson, Jamie L., Erik J. Engstrom, and Jason M. Roberts. 2007. "Candidate Quality, the Personal Vote, and the Incumbency Advantage in Congress." *American Political Science Review* 101 (2): 289–301.

Carson, Jamie L., Spencer Hardin, and Aaron Hitefield. 2021. "You're Fired! Donald Trump and the 2020 Congressional Elections." *The Forum* 18 (4): 627–650.

Carson, Jamie L., and M. V. Hood III. 2014. "Candidates, Competition, and the Partisan Press: Congressional Elections in the Early Antebellum Era." *American Politics Research* 42 (5): 760–783.

Carson, Jamie L., and Jeffery A. Jenkins. 2011. "Examining the Electoral Connection across Time." *Annual Review of Political Science* 14: 25–46.

Carson, Jamie L., Gregory Koger, Matthew J. Lebo, and Everett Young. 2010. "The Electoral Costs of Party Loyalty in Congress." *American Journal of Political Science* 54 (3): 598–616.

Carson, Jamie L., and Stephen Pettigrew. 2013. "Strategic Politicians, Partisan Roll Calls, and the Tea Party: Evaluating the 2010 Midterm Elections." *Electoral Studies* 32 (1): 26–36.

Carson, Jamie L., and Jason M. Roberts. 2013. *Ambition, Competition, and Electoral Reform: The Politics of Congressional Elections across Time*. Ann Arbor: University of Michigan Press.

Carson, Jamie L., and Joel Sievert. 2017. "Congressional Candidates in the Era of Party Ballots." *Journal of Politics* 79 (2): 534–545.

Carson, Jamie L., and Joel Sievert. 2018. *Electoral Incentives in Congress*. Ann Arbor: University of Michigan Press.

Carson, Jamie L., Joel Sievert, and Ryan D. Williamson. 2020. "Nationalization and the Incumbency Advantage." *Political Research Quarterly* 73 (1): 156–168.

Carson, Jamie L., and Ryan D. Williamson. 2018a. "Candidate Emergence in the Era of Direct Primaries." In *Handbook of Primary Elections,* ed. Robert Boatright, 57–71. New York: Routledge.

Carson, Jamie L., and Ryan D. Williamson. 2018b. "Candidate Ideology and Electoral Success in Congressional Elections." *Public Choice* 176: 175–192.

Caughey, Devin, and Jasjeet S. Sekhon. 2011. "Elections and the Regression Discontinuity Design: Lessons from Close U.S. House Races, 1942–2008." *Political Analysis* 19: 385–408.

Chhibber, Predeep, and Ken Kollman. 2004. *The Formation of National Party Systems: Federalism and Party Competition in Canada, Great Britain, India, and the United States.* Princeton, NJ: Princeton University Press.

Claggett, William. 1987. "The Nationalization of Congressional Turnout: A Research Note." *Western Political Quarterly* 40 (3): 527–533.

Claggett, William, William Flanigan, and Nancy Zingale. 1984. "Nationalization of the American Electorate." *American Political Science Review* 78 (1): 77–91.

Cover, Albert D. 1977. "One Good Term Deserves Another: The Advantage of Incumbency in Congressional Elections." *American Journal of Political Science* 21: 523–541.

Cover, Albert D., and Bruce S. Brumberg. 1982. "Baby Books and Ballots: The Impact of Congressional Mail on Constituency Opinion." *American Political Science Review* 76: 347–359.

Cox, Gary W., and Jonathan N. Katz. 1996. "Why Did the Incumbency Advantage in U.S. House Elections Grow?" *American Journal of Political Science* 40: 478–497.

Dahl, Robert A. 1971. *Polyarchy: Participation and Opposition.* New Haven, CT: Yale University Press.

Dancey, Logan, and Geoffrey Sheagley. 2016. "Inferences Made Easy: Partisan Voting in Congress, Voter Awareness, and Senator Approval." *American Politics Research* 44 (50): 844–874.

Dancey, Logan, Matthew Tarpey, and Jonathan Woon. 2019. "The Macro-dynamics of Partisan Advantage." *Political Research Quarterly* 72 (2): 450–459.

Davis, Nicholas T., and Lilliana Mason. 2016. "Sorting and the Split-Ticket: Evidence from Presidential and Subpresidential Elections." *Political Behavior* 38: 337–354.

de la Cuesta, Brandon, and Kosuke Imai. 2016. "Misunderstandings about the Regression Discontinuity Design in the Study of Close Elections." *Annual Review of Political Science* 19: 375–196.

Drutman, Lee. 2018. "America Has Local Political Institutions but National Politics. This Is a Problem." *Vox*, May 31.

Dubin, Michael J. 1998. *United States Congressional Elections, 1788–1997: The Official Results of the Elections of the 1st through 105th Congresses.* Jefferson, NC: McFarland.

Eggers, Andrew C., Anthony Fowler, Jens Hainmueller, Andrew B. Hall, and James M. Snyder Jr. 2015. "On the Validity of the Regression Discontinuity Design for Estimating Electoral Effects: New Evidence from over 40,000 Close Races." *American Journal of Political Science* 59 (1): 259–274.

Elder, Elizabeth Mitchell, and Neil A. O'Brian. 2022. "Social Groups as the Source of Political Belief Systems: Fresh Evidence on an Old Theory." *American Political Science Review* 116 (4): 1407–1424.

Engstrom, Erik J. 2012. "The Rise and Decline of Turnout in Congressional Elections: Electoral Institutions, Competition, and Strategic Mobilization." *American Journal of Political Science* 56 (April): 373–386.

Engstrom, Erik J., and Samuel Kernell. 2005. "Manufactured Responsiveness: The Impact of State Electoral Laws on Unified Control of the Presidency and House of Representatives, 1840–1940." *American Journal of Political Science* 49 (3): 531–549.

Engstrom, Erik J., and Samuel Kernell. 2014. *Party Ballots, Reform, and the Transformation of America's Electoral System*. New York: Cambridge University Press.

Erikson, Robert S. 1971. "The Advantage of Incumbency in Congressional Elections." *Polity* 3 (3): 395–405.

Erikson, Robert S. 1972. "Malapportionment, Gerrymandering, and Party Fortunes." *American Political Science Review* 66: 1234–1245.

Erikson, Robert S. 2016. "The Congressional Incumbency Advantage over Sixty Years: Measurement, Trends, and Implications." In *Governing in a Polarized Age*, eds. Alan S. Gerber and Eric Schickler, 65–89. New York: Cambridge University Press.

Erikson, Robert S., and Kelly Rader. 2017. "Much Ado about Nothing: RDD and the Incumbency Advantage." *Political Analysis* 24 (2): 269–275.

Erikson, Robert S., and Rocio Titiunik. 2015. "Using Regression Discontinuity to Uncover the Personal Incumbency Advantage." *Quarterly Journal of Political Science* 10 (1): 101–119.

Fenno, Richard F. 1978. *Home Style: House Members in Their Districts*. New York: Longman.

Ferejohn, John A. 1977. "On the Decline of Competition in Congressional Elections." *American Political Science Review* 71: 166–176.

Finkel, Steven E. 1995. *Causal Analysis with Panel Data*. Thousand Oaks, CA: Sage.

Finocchiaro, Charles J., and Jeffery A. Jenkins. 2016. "Distributive Politics, the Electoral Connection, and the Antebellum U.S. Congress: The Case of Military Service Pensions." *Journal of Theoretical Politics* 28 (2): 192–224.

Finocchiaro, Charles J., and Scott A. MacKenzie. 2018. "Making Washington Work: Legislative Entrepreneurship and the Personal Vote from the Gilded Age to the Great Depression." *American Journal of Political Science* 62: 113–131.

Fiorina, Morris P. 1977. "The Case of the Vanishing Marginals: The Bureaucracy Did It." *American Political Science Review* 71: 177–181.

Fiorina, Morris P. 2016. "The (Re)Nationalization of Congressional Elections." Hoover Institution Essay on Contemporary American Politics. Stanford, CA: Stanford University.

Fiorina, Morris, David Rohde, and Peter Wissel. 1975. "Historical Change in House Turnover." In *Congress in Change*, ed. Norman Ornstein, 24–57. New York: Praeger.

Formisano, Ronald P. 1974. "Deferential-Participant Politics: The Early Republic's Political Culture, 1789–1840." *American Political Science Review* 68 (June): 473–487.

Fouirnaies, Alexander, and Andrew B. Hall. 2014. "The Financial Incumbency Advantage: Causes and Consequences." *Journal of Politics* 76 (3): 711–724.

Fulton, Sarah A., Cherie D. Maestas, L. Sandy Maisel, and Walter J. Stone. 2006. "The Sense of a Woman: Gender, Ambition, and the Decision to Run for Congress." *Political Research Quarterly* 59 (2): 235–248.

Garand, James C., and Donald A. Gross. 1984. "Trends in the Vote Margins for Congressional Candidates: A Specification of Historical Trends." *American Political Science Review* 78 (1): 17–30.

Gartner, Scott Sigmund, Gary M. Segura, and Bethany A. Barratt. 2003. "War Casualties, Policy Positions, and the Fate of Legislators." *Political Research Quarterly* 55 (3): 467–477.

Gelman, Andrew, and Gary King. 1990. "Estimating Incumbency Advantage without Bias." *American Journal of Political Science* 34: 1142–1164.

Gilmour, John B., and Paul Rothstein. 1993. "Early Republican Retirement: A Cause of Democratic Dominance in the House of Representatives." *Legislative Studies Quarterly* 18 (3): 345–365.

Gimpel, James G., Frances E. Lee, and Shanna Pearson-Merkowitz. 2008. "The Check Is in the Mail: Interdistrict Funding Flows in Congressional Elections." *American Journal of Political Science* 52 (April): 373–394.

Green, Donald Philip, and Jonathan S. Krasno. 1988. "Salvation for the Spendthrift Incumbent: Reestimating the Effects of Campaign Spending in House Elections." *American Journal of Political Science* 32 (November): 884–907.

Grier, Kevin B., and Joseph P. McGarrity. 2002. "Presidential Party, Incumbency, and the Effects of Economic Fluctuations on House Elections, 1916–1996." *Public Choice* 110 (1–2): 143–162.

Grofman, Bernard, William Koetzle, Michael P. McDonald, and Thomas L. Brunell. 2000. "A New Look at Split-Ticket Outcomes for House and President: The Comparative Midpoints Model." *Journal of Politics* 62 (1): 34–50.

Groseclose, Timothy, and Keith Krehbiel. 1994. "Golden Parachutes, Rubber Checks, and Strategic Retirements from the 102d House." *American Journal of Political Science* 38 (1): 75–99.

Gross, Donald A., and James C. Garand. 1984. "The Vanishing Marginals, 1824–1980." *Journal of Politics* 46 (1): 224–237.

Hainmueller, Jens, Andrew B. Hall, and James M. Snyder Jr. 2015. "Assessing the External Validity of Election RD Estimates: An Investigation of the Incumbency Advantage." *Journal of Politics* 77 (3): 707–720.

Hall, Andrew B. 2019. *Who Wants to Run? How the Devaluing of Political Office Drives Polarization*. Chicago: University of Chicago Press.

Hall, Richard L., and Robert P. van Houweling. 1995. "Avarice and Ambition in Congress: Representatives' Decision to Run or Retire from the U.S. House." *American Political Science Review* 89 (1): 121–136.

Hare, Christopher, and Keith T. Poole. 2014. "The Polarization of Contemporary American Politics." *Polity* 46 (3): 411–429.

Herrnson, Paul S. 2012. *Congressional Elections: Campaigning at Home and in Washington*. Washington, DC: CQ Press.

Hetherington, Mark J. 2001. "Resurgent Mass Partisanship: The Role of Elite Polarization." *American Political Science Review* 95: 619–631.

Hibbing, John R. 1982a. "Voluntary Retirement from the U.S. House of Representatives: Who Quits?" *American Journal of Political Science* 26 (3): 467–484.

Hibbing, John R. 1982b. "Voluntary Retirement from the U.S. House: The Costs of Congressional Service." *Legislative Studies Quarterly* 7 (1): 57–74.

Hibbing, John R., and John R. Alford. 1981. "The Electoral Impact of Economic Conditions: Who Is Held Responsible?" *American Journal of Political Science* 25 (3): 423–439.

Highton, Benjamin. 2002. "Bill Clinton, Newt Gingrich, and the 1998 House Elections." *Public Opinion Quarterly* 66 (1): 1–17.

Hinckley, Barbara. 1980. "House Re-elections and Senate Defeats: The Role of the Challenger." *British Journal of Political Science* 10: 441–460.

Hirano, Shigeo, James M. Snyder Jr., Stephen Ansolabehere, and John Mark Hansen. 2010. "Primary Elections and Partisan Polarization in the U.S. Congress." *Quarterly Journal of Political Science* 5 (2): 169–191.

Hopkins, Daniel J. 2018. *The Increasingly United States: How and Why American Political Behavior Nationalized*. Chicago: University of Chicago Press.

Hopkins, Daniel J., and Hans Noel. 2022. "Trump and the Shifting Meaning of 'Conservative': Using Activists' Pairwise Comparisons to Measure Politicians' Perceived Ideologies." *American Political Science Review* 116 (3): 1133–1140.

Jacobson, Gary C. 1987. "The Marginals Never Vanished: Incumbency and Competition in Elections to the U.S. House of Representatives, 1952–82." *American Journal of Political Science* 43 (4): 1042–1061.

Jacobson, Gary C. 1989. "Strategic Politicians and the Dynamics of U.S. House Elections, 1946–86." *American Political Science Review* 83 (September): 773–793.

Jacobson, Gary C. 1990. *The Electoral Origins of Divided Government: Competition in U.S. House Elections, 1946–1988*. Boulder: Westview Press.

Jacobson, Gary C. 1993. "Getting the Details Right: A Comment on 'Changing Meanings of Electoral Marginality in U.S. House Elections, 1824–1978.'" *Political Research Quarterly* 46 (1): 49–54.

Jacobson, Gary C. 1996. "The 1994 House Elections in Perspective." *Political Science Quarterly* 111 (Summer): 203–223.

Jacobson, Gary C. 2000. "Party Polarization in National Politics: The Electoral Connection." In *Polarized Politics: Congress and the President in a Partisan Era*, eds. Jon R. Bond and Richard Fleisher, 9–30. Washington, DC: Congressional Quarterly Press.

Jacobson, Gary C. 2007. "Referendum: The 2006 Midterm Elections." *Political Science Quarterly* 122 (1): 1–24.

Jacobson, Gary C. 2011. "The Republican Resurgence in 2010." *Political Science Quarterly* 126 (1): 27–52.

Jacobson, Gary C. 2015a. "Barack Obama and the Nationalization of Electoral Politics in 2012." *Electoral Studies* 40: 471–481.

Jacobson, Gary C. 2015b. "It's Nothing Personal: The Decline of the Incumbency Advantage in Congressional Elections." *Journal of Politics* 77 (July): 861–873.

Jacobson, Gary C. 2015c. "Obama and Nationalized Electoral Politics in the 2014 Midterm." *Political Science Quarterly* 130 (1): 1–25.

Jacobson, Gary C. 2017. "The Triumph of Polarized Partisanship in 2016: Donald Trump's Improbable Victory." *Political Science Quarterly* 132 (1): 9–41.

Jacobson, Gary C. 2019a. "Extreme Referendum: Donald Trump and the 2018 Midterm Elections." *Political Science Quarterly* 134 (1): 9–38.

Jacobson, Gary C. 2019b. *Presidents and Parties in the Public Mind*. Chicago: University of Chicago Press.

Jacobson, Gary C. 2020. "Donald Trump and the Parties: Impeachment, Pandemic, Protest, and Electoral Politics in 2020." *Presidential Studies Quarterly* 50 (4): 762–795.

Jacobson, Gary C. 2021. "The Presidential and Congressional Elections of 2020: A National Referendum on the Trump Presidency." *Political Science Quarterly* 136 (1): 11–45.

Jacobson, Gary C., and Jamie L. Carson. 2020. *The Politics of Congressional Elections*. 10th edition. Lanham, MD: Rowman & Littlefield.

Jacobson, Gary C., and Samuel Kernell. 1983. *Strategy and Choice in Congressional Elections*. New Haven, CT: Yale University Press.

Jenkins, Jeffery, Eric Schickler, and Jamie Carson. 2004. "Constituency Cleavages and Congressional Parties: Measuring Homogeneity and Polarization, 1857–1913." *Social Science History* 28 (4): 537–573.

Johannes, John R., and John C. McAdams. 1981. "The Congressional Incumbency Effect: Is It Casework, Policy Compatibility, or Something Else?" *American Journal of Political Science* 25: 520–542.

Karol, David, and Edward Miguel. 2007. "The Electoral Cost of War: Iraq Casualties and the 2004 U.S. Presidential Election." *Journal of Politics* 69 (3): 633–648.

Kaslovsky, Jaclyn. 2022. "Senators at Home: Local Attentiveness and Policy Representation in Congress." *American Political Science Review* 116 (2): 645–661.

Katz, Jonathan M., and Brian R Sala. 1996. "Careerism, Committee Assignments, and the Electoral Connection." *American Political Science Review* 90 (1): 21–33.

Katz, Richard S. 1973. "The Attribution of Variance in Electoral Returns: An Alternative Measurement Technique." *American Political Science Review* 67 (3): 817–828.

Kawato, Sadafumi. 1987. "Nationalization and Partisan Realignment in Congressional Elections." *American Political Science Review* 81 (4): 1235–1250.

Kernell, Samuel. 1977a. "Presidential Popularity and Negative Voting: An Alternative Explanation of the Midterm Congressional Decline of the President's Party." *American Political Science Review* 71 (1): 44–66.

Kernell, Samuel. 1977b. "Toward Understanding 19th Century Congressional Careers: Ambition, Competition, and Rotation." *American Journal of Political Science* 21: 669–693.

Kernell, Samuel. 2003. "The True Principles of Republican Government: Reassessing James Madison's Political Science." In *James Madison: The Theory and Practice of Republican Government*, ed. Samuel Kernell, 92–125. Palo Alto, CA: Stanford University Press.

Key, V. O., Jr. 1966. *The Responsible Electorate*. Cambridge, MA: Belknap Press of Harvard University.

Kiewiet, D. Roderick, and Langche Zeng. 1993. "An Analysis of Congressional Career Decision, 1947–1986." *American Political Science Review* 87 (4): 928–941.

Knotts, H. Gibbs, and Jordan M. Ragusa. 2016. "The Nationalization of Special Elections for the U.S. House of Representatives." *Journal of Elections, Public Opinion and Parties* 26 (1): 22–39.

Krasno, Jonathan S. 1994. *Challengers, Competition, and Reelection: Comparing Senate and House Elections*. New Haven, CT: Yale University Press.

Kriner, Douglas L., and Francis X. Shen. 2007. "Iraq Casualties and the 2006 Senate Elections." *Legislative Studies Quarterly* 32 (4): 507–530.

Ladewig, Jeffrey W. 2010. "Ideological Polarization and the Vanishing of Marginals: Retrospective Roll-Call Voting in the U.S. Congress." *Journal of Politics* 72 (2): 499–512.

Lee, David S. 2008. "Randomized Experiments from Non-Random Selection in U.S. House Elections." *Journal of Econometrics* 142: 675–697.

Lee, Frances E. 2009. *Beyond Ideology: Political, Principles, and Partisanship in the US Senate*. Chicago: University of Chicago Press.

Lee, Frances E. 2016. *Insecure Majorities: Congress and the Perpetual Campaign*. Chicago: University of Chicago Press.

Levendusky, Matthew. 2009. *The Partisan Sort: How Liberals Became Democrats and Conservatives Became Republicans*. Chicago: University of Chicago Press.

Lewis, Verlan. 2021. "The Problem of Donald Trump and the Statis Spectrum Fallacy." *Party Politics* 27 (4): 605–618.

Lynch, G. Patrick. 2002. "Midterm Elections and Economic Fluctuations: The Response of Voters over Time." *Legislative Studies Quarterly* 27 (2): 265–294.

MacKenzie, Scott A. 2015. "Life before Congress: Using Pre-congressional Experience to Assess Competing Explanations for Political Professionalism." *Journal of Politics* 77 (2): 505–518.

Maestas, Cherie, Sarah A. Fulton, L. Sandy Maisel, and Walter J. Stone. 2006. "When to Risk It? Institutions, Ambitions, and the Decision to Run for the U.S. House." *American Political Science Review* 100 (May): 195–208.

Mann, Thomas E., and Raymond E. Wolfinger. 1980. "Candidates and Parties in Congressional Elections." *American Political Science Review* 74 (3): 617–632.

Martin, Danielle Joesten. 2022. "Ideological and Partisan Biases in Ratings of Candidate Quality in US House Elections." *Social Science Quarterly* 103 (3): 622–634.

Martin, Gregory J., and Joshua McCrain. 2019. "Local News and National Politics." *American Political Science Review* 113 (2): 372–384.

Martis, Kenneth C. 1989. *The Historical Atlas of Political Parties in the United States, 1789–1989*. New York: Macmillan.

Mason, Lilliana. 2018. *Uncivil Agreement: How Politics Become Our Identity*. Chicago: University of Chicago Press.

Mayhew, David R. 1974a. "Congressional Elections: The Case of the Vanishing Marginals." *Polity* 6: 295–317.

Mayhew, David R. 1974b. *Congress: The Electoral Connection*. New Haven, CT: Yale University Press.

McCarty, Nolan, Keith T. Poole, and Howard Rosenthal. 2009. "Does Gerrymandering Cause Polarization?" *American Journal of Political Science* 53 (3): 666–680.

McCarty, Nolan, Keith T. Poole, and Howard Rosenthal. 2016. *Polarized America: The Dance of Ideology and Unequal Riches*. 2nd edition. Cambridge, MA: MIT Press.

McCurley, Carl, and Jeffery J. Mondak. 1995. "Inspected by #1184063113: The Influence of Incumbents' Competence and Integrity in US House Elections." *American Journal of Political Science* 39 (4): 864–885.

McDermott, Monika L. 2006. "Not for Members Only: Group Endorsements as Electoral Information Cues." *Political Research Quarterly* 59 (2): 249–257.

Melusky, Benjamin, and Jesse Richman. 2020. "When the Local Is National—A New High- water Mark for Nationalization in the 2018 United States State Legislative Elections." *Regional & Federal Studies* 30 (3): 441–460.

Merrill, Samuel, III, Bernard Grofman, and Thomas L. Brunell. 2014. "Modeling the Electoral Dynamics of Party Polarization in Two-Party Legislatures." *Journal of Theoretical Politics* 26 (4): 548–572.

Milita, Kerri, Elizabeth N. Simas, John Barry Ryan, and Yanna Krupnikov. 2017. "The Effects of Ambiguous Rhetoric in Congressional Elections." *Electoral Studies* 46: 48–63.

Miller, Arthur H., Christopher Wlezien, and Anne Hildreth. 1991. "A Reference Group Theory of Partisan Coalitions." *Journal of Politics* 53 (4): 1134–1149.

Mondak, Jeffery J. 1995. "Competence, Integrity, and the Electoral Success of Congressional Incumbents." *Journal of Politics* 57 (4): 1043–1069.

Morgenstern, Scott, Stephen M. Swindle, and Andrea Castagnola. 2009. "Party Nationalization and Institutions." *Journal of Politics* 71 (4): 1322–1341.

Moskowitz, Daniel J. 2021. "Local News, Information, and the Nationalization of U.S. Elections." *American Political Science Review* 115 (1): 114–129.

Nicholson, Stephen P. 2011. "Polarizing Cues." *American Journal of Political Science* 56 (1): 52–66.

Niemi, Richard, Simon Jackman, and Laura Winsky. 1991. "Candidacies and Competitiveness in Multimember Districts." *Legislative Studies Quarterly* 16: 91–109.

Oppenheimer, Bruce I., James A. Stimson, and Richard Waterman. 1986. "Interpreting U.S. Congressional Elections: The Exposure Thesis." *Legislative Studies Quarterly* 11 (2): 227–247.

Polsby, Nelson W. 1968. "The Institutionalization of the U.S. House of Representatives." *American Political Science Review* 62: 144–168.

Poole, Keith T., and Howard Rosenthal. 1984. "The Polarization of American Politics." *Journal of Politics* 46 (4): 1061–1079.

Poole, Keith T., and Howard Rosenthal. 2007. *Ideology and Congress*. New Brunswick, NJ: Transaction.

Price, H. Douglas. 1975. "Congress and the Evolution of Legislative 'Professionalism.'" In *Congress in Change: Evolution and Reform*, ed. Norman J. Ornstein, 2–23. New York: Praeger Publishers, Inc.

Prior, Markus. 2007. *Post-Broadcast Democracy: How Media Choice Increases Inequality in Political Involvement and Polarizes Elections*. New York: Cambridge University Press.

Rahn, Wendy M. 1993. "The Role of Partisan Stereotypes in Information Processing about Political Candidates." *American Journal of Political Science* 37 (2): 472–496.

Reckhow, Sarah, Jeffrey R. Henig, Rebecca Jacobsen, and Jamie Alter Litt. 2017. "'Outsiders with Deep Pockets': The Nationalization of Local School Board Elections." *Urban Affairs Review* 53 (5): 783–811.

Reynolds, John F. 2006. *The Demise of the American Convention System, 1880 – 1911*. New York: Cambridge University Press.

Reynolds, Molly E. 2017. "Retirement from Congress May Be Driven by Term Limits on Committee chairs." Report. Washington, DC: Brookings Institution.

Roberts, Jason M., Jacob F. H. Smith, and Sarah A. Treul. 2016. "Party Committee Targeting and the Evolution of Competition in US House Elections." *Journal of Elections, Public Opinion and Parties* 26 (1): 96–114.

Rogers, Steven. 2016. "National Forces in State Legislative Elections." *Annals of the American Academy of Political and Social Science* 667 (1): 207–225.

Rogowski, Jon C., and Patrick D. Tucker. 2018. "Moderate, Extreme, or Both? How Voters Respond to Ideologically Unpredictable Candidates." *Electoral Studies* 51: 83–92.

Rusk, Jerrold G. 1970. "The Effects of the Australian Ballot Reform on Split Ticket Voting: 1876–1908." *American Political Science Review* 64 (December): 1220–1238.

Schattschneider, E. E. 1960. *The Semisovereign People: A Realist's View of Democracy in America*. New York: Holt, Reinhart, and Winston.

Sievert, Joel, and Kevin Banda. 2022. "All Politics Is National: Partisan Defection in National and Subnational Elections." Unpublished manuscript.

Sievert, Joel, and Victor Hinojosa. 2022. "Whose Party Is It? Lame Ducks, Presidential Candidates, and Evaluations of the Party." *American Politics Research* 50 (4): 539–544.

Sievert, Joel, and Stephanie Mathiasen. 2023. "Out-of-State Donors and Nationalized Politics in U.S. Senate Elections." *The Forum*. Forthcoming.

Sievert, Joel, and Seth C. McKee. 2019. "Nationalization in U.S. Senate and Gubernatorial Elections." *American Politics Research* 47 (5): 1055–1080.

Sievert, Joel, and Ryan D. Williamson. 2018. "Public Attitudes toward Presidential Veto Powers." *Research & Politics* 5 (1): 2053168017753873.

Sievert, Joel, and Ryan D. Williamson. 2022. "Elections, Competition, and Constituent Evaluations of US Senators." *Electoral Studies* 75: 102424.

Simas, Elizabeth N. 2018. "Perceptions of the Heterogeneity of Party Elites in the United States." *Party Politics* 24 (4): 444–454.

Simas, Elizabeth N. 2020. "Extremely High Quality? How Ideology Shapes Perceptions of Candidates' Personal Traits." *Public Opinion Quarterly* 84 (3): 699–724.

Simon, Dennis M. 1989. "Presidents, Governors, and Electoral Accountability." *Journal of Politics* 51: 286–304.

Skeen, C. Edward. 1986. "*Vox Populi, Vox Dei:* The Compensation Act of 1816 and the Rise of Popular Politics." *Journal of the Early Republic* 6 (Autumn): 253–274.

Smidt, Corwin. 2017. "Polarization and the Decline of the American Floating Voter." *American Journal of Political Science* 61 (2): 365–381.

Stephens-Dougan, LaFleur. 2020. *Race to the Bottom: How Racial Appeals Work in American Politics*. Chicago: University of Chicago Press.

Stokes, Donald E. 1965. "A Variance Components Model of Political Effects." In *Mathematical Applications in Political Science*, ed. J. M. Claunch, 61–85. Dallas, TX: Arnold Foundation.

Stokes, Donald E. 1967. "Parties and the Nationalization of Electoral Forces." In *The American Party Systems*, eds. W. N. Chambers and W. D. Burnham, 182–202. New York: Oxford University Press.

Stone, Walter J., and Elizabeth N. Simas. 2010. "Candidate Valence and Ideological Positions in US House Elections." *American Journal of Political Science* 54 (2): 371–388.

Stonecash, Jeffrey M. 2008. *Reassessing the Incumbency Effect*. New York: Cambridge University Press.

# References

Swift, Elaine K. 1987. "The Electoral Connection Meets the Past: Lessons from Congressional History, 1789–1899." *Political Science Quarterly* 102 (4): 625–645.

Tesler, Michael. 2016. *Post-Racial or Most-Racial? Race and Politics in the Obama Era.* Chicago: University of Chicago Press.

Theriault, Sean M. 2006. "Party Polarization in the U.S. Congress: Member Replacement and Member Adaptation." *Party Politics* 12 (4): 483–503.

Theriault, Sean M. 2008. *Party Polarization in Congress.* New York: Cambridge University Press.

Theriault, Sean M. 2013. *The Gingrich Senators.* Oxford: Oxford University Press.

Thomsen, Danielle M. 2014. "Ideological Moderates Won't Run: How Party Fit Matters for Partisan Polarization in Congress." *Journal of Politics* 76 (3): 786–797.

Thomsen, Danielle M. 2017. *Opting Out of Congress: Partisan Polarization and the Decline of Moderate Candidates.* New York: Cambridge University Press.

Trussler, Marc. 2021. "Get Information or Get in Formation: The Effects of High-Information Environments on Legislative Elections." *British Journal of Political Science* 51: 1529–1549.

Tufte, Edward R. 1973. "The Relationship between Seats and Votes in Two-Party Systems." *American Political Science Review* 67 (June): 540–554.

Tufte, Edward R. 1975. "Determinants of the Outcomes of Midterm Congressional Elections." *American Political Science Review* 69 (3): 812–826.

Vertz, Laura L., John P. Frendreis, and James L. Gibson. 1987. "Nationalization of the Electorate in the United States." *American Political Science Review* 81 (3): 961–966.

Ware, Alan. 2002. *The American Direct Primary: Party Institutionalization and Transformation in the North.* New York: Cambridge University Press.

Weinschenk, Arron, Mandi Baker, Zoe Betancourt, Vanessa Depies, Nathan Erck, Quinne Herolt, Amanda Loehrke, Cameron Makurat, Hannah Malmberg, Clarice Martell, Jared Novitzke, Bradley Riddle, Tara Sellen, Leah Tauferner, and Emily Zilliox. 2020. "Have State Supreme Court Elections Nationalized?" *Justice System Journal* 41 (4): 313–322.

Wilkins, Arjun S. 2012. "Electoral Security of Members of the U.S. House, 1900–2006." *Legislative Studies Quarterly* 37 (3): 277–304.

Williamson, Ryan D. 2019. "Evaluating Candidate Positioning and Success in the 2018 Midterm Elections." *The Forum* 16 (4): 675–686.

Zingher, Joshua N., and Jesse Richman. 2019. "Polarization and the Nationalization of State Legislative Elections." *American Politics Research* 47 (5): 1036–1054.

# INDEX

*For the benefit of digital users, indexed terms that span two pages (e.g., 52–53) may, on occasion, appear on only one of those pages.*

25th Amendment, 127

abortion, 153–54
Abrams, Stacey, 154
accountability, 8, 11, 26–27, 41, 42–55, 61–62, 92–93, 101, 150–53, 156, 160
Affordable Care Act, 2–3, 23–24
Alabama, 12–13, 19–20, 139–41
Alexander, Lamar, 139–40
Allred, Colin, 65
ambition, 24–25, 41, 56, 114
American National Election Study (ANES), 118, 120, 122–23, 128–29, 131, 132
approval, 1, 7–8, 15, 18–19, 56, 124, 128, 151, 154–55
Arizona, 142–43
Australian ballot, 4, 5–6, 25–27, 44, 83, 91, 158

Biden, Joseph, 7–8, 114, 133–37, 140–42, 143, 144–45, 146, 148–49, 150, 151, 153–56
Big Business, 120, 121, 122–23
Big Lie. *See* election denialism
Black Lives Matter, 12–13
Boebert, Lauren, 163
Boehner, John, 95

Brat, David, 95–96
Britt, Katie, 19–20
Brooks, Mo, 19–20
Bush, George H.W., 6
Bush, George W., 6, 152

California, 152–53
Cantor, Eric, 95–96
Cawthorn, Madison, 161–62
challengers, 1, 56, 66–67, 68, 72, 74, 117, 132, 137–38, 141–42, 154
Christian Fundamentalist, 120–21
Ciattarelli, Jack, 154–55
Civil Rights Act, 66
climate change, 153–54
Clinton, Bill, 1–2, 6
Clinton, Hillary, 64–65, 126–27, 141
coattails, 5, 27, 38–39, 45, 50–52
Collins, Susan, 141–42, 143
Colorado, 163
competence, 117, 124–26
competition/competitiveness, 4–5, 13–14, 27, 48–49, 53–54, 64–65, 66, 87, 88, 91, 95, 96–97, 98, 99, 101–5, 106, 110, 112, 113, 119–20, 142–43, 144, 146–48, 150, 152–53
Cooperative Election Study (CES), 124–26, 128–29, 131, 132

COVID, 7–8, 151–53, 155–56
cues. *See* heuristics
Cuomo, Andrew, 152–53

Davis, Rodney, 8
defund the police, 12–13
Democratic Congressional Campaign Committee (DCCC), 133–34, 135–37
depolarization, 110
direct primary, 4, 25–27, 44, 91, 98–99
down-ticket/down-ballot, 3–4, 5–6, 11, 17, 150, 155, 162
Duncan, Geoff, 162
Durant, Mike, 19–20
Durr Jr., Edward, 155

economy, 7–8, 15–16, 23–24, 43, 56, 120–21, 122–23, 137, 152, 153–54
Edwards, Chuck, 161–62
election denialism, 19–21, 126–27, 153–54, 163
election timing, 44–55, 83–90, 158
electoral college, 23, 143, 153
elites, 4–5, 21, 56, 158
endorsements, 11, 19–20, 114, 116–17, 132–37, 143, 145–50, 153–54, 156, 159, 161–62

Feminists, 122–23
Frisch, Adam, 163

Gays and Lesbians, 120–21
Georgia, 142–43, 150, 154, 162
gerrymandering, 98–99
Gideon, Sara, 143
Gingrich, Newt, 1, 65–66
governors, 19, 152–53, 162
Grant, Ulysses S., 23, 24
Greeley, Horace, 23
gridlock, 10, 67
gubernatorial elections, 2–3, 11, 15, 19, 153–55

Harris, Kamala, 143, 154–55
heuristics, 115, 116–17, 120, 132–33, 137

ideology:
    congruity, 10, 106–7
    extremity, 11, 97, 99, 100, 102, 106–7, 110
    moderation, 10, 92, 97, 100, 106–7, 112, 139–40, 144, 163
Illinois, 24–25, 65–66
income inequality, 94, 98, 99, 107, 113
incumbency advantage:
    direct effect, 74–75, 81–82, 83, 84–86, 90
    indirect effect, 74, 75, 80, 81–83, 85–86, 90
    personal, 76, 78, 79–82, 92
    partisan, 78, 79–80
    quality effect, 74, 75, 80, 83
    scare-off effect, 68, 72, 74, 75, 76, 80–81, 82, 83, 92
institutional design, 9, 39, 91
integrity, 117, 124–26
interest groups, 116–17
Iowa, 114, 150

Jones, Doug, 139–41
Jones, Joyce, 12–13

Kemp, Brian, 162

Labor Unions, 120, 121, 122–23
legislative agenda, 145–46
legislative process/procedure/politics, 94, 97, 156
Lewis, Ron, 1–2
Lincoln, Abraham, 24–26
loyalty, 2, 9, 10, 22, 70–71, 95, 100–1, 105–6, 110, 112

Maine, 2, 141–42, 143–44, 150
Mandel, Josh, 20
McAuliffe, Terry, 153–55
McCarthy, Kevin, 126–27
McDonnell, Bob, 153
Meadows, Mark, 161–62
Michel, Robert, 65–67
Michigan, 142–43

# Index

midterm, 5, 6–7, 23–24, 28–30, 35–36, 37–39, 42–43, 44–45, 46–50, 55–56, 57–59, 61–62, 64, 71–72, 84–85, 89–90, 102–3, 109–10, 126–27, 145–46, 160
mobilization, 115, 139, 150, 154, 161
money, 68, 94–95, 140, 160–62
Montana, 150
Moore, Roy, 139
Murphy, Phil, 154–55

Natcher, William, 1–2
National Republican Campaign Committee (NRCC), 133–36
New Hampshire, 114
New Jersey, 153, 154–55
Newsome, Gavin, 152–53
New York, 152–53
nominating convention, 26–27, 107
Northam, Ralph, 153
North Carolina, 142–43, 150

Obama, Barack, 2–3, 6, 23–24, 129–31, 143, 154–55
Obamacare. *See* Affordable Care Act
Ohio, 19–20
O'Neill, Tip, 12, 66
open seat, 34, 48–49, 52–54, 61–62, 78–79
Oregon, 144

pandemic. *See* COVID
partisan/national tides, 43, 48–52, 53–54, 58, 67, 156
party ballot, 2, 4, 5, 8, 9, 22, 26–27, 28, 35–36, 38–40, 43–44, 46, 55, 62–63, 71–72, 73, 83–84, 87–90, 107, 109, 111–12, 137, 158, 159
party brand, 39, 94–95, 116, 133–34, 137–38, 144, 154–55
party leaders/leadership, 6–7, 42, 65–66, 94, 95–96, 97, 107, 115–16, 120, 137, 162
Pelosi, Nancy, 6–7, 65
Pence, Mike, 42
Perdue, David, 162

Pingree, Chellie, 143
polarization, 4–5, 9, 10, 17–18, 21, 69–70, 73, 94–113, 143–44, 159
Police, 122–23
poor, 122–23
Prather, Joe, 1–2
primary elections, 19–20, 65, 95–96, 97, 98–99, 162
Progressive Era, 4, 5–6, 27, 44, 160–61, 163–64
public opinion/public evaluations, 39, 56, 122

quality challengers, 27, 50, 71–72, 74–75, 76, 80–81, 83, 115, 136–37, 146, 148–49

racial groups, 120–23
Reagan, Ronald, 6, 118–19
reapportionment, 30–31, 78–79
redistricting, 30–31, 34, 57, 68, 98
regression discontinuity design (RDD), 76, 78–79
replacement, 68, 94–95, 97, 98, 99, 100, 110
representation, 8, 66–67, 71–72, 110–12
responsiveness, 41, 100, 135, 140–41, 145–46
retirements, 46, 48, 49–50, 52–54, 56–63, 65–66
rich, 122–23
Rostenkowski, Dan, 66

scandal, 57, 161–62
scare-off, 68, 71–83, 92
Schrader, Kurt, 144
secretaries of state, 20–21
Sessions, Jeff, 139
Sessions, Pete, 64–65
Shelby, Richard, 19–20, 139
South Carolina, 114, 150
Southern Strategy, 5–6
Spanberger, Abigail, 144
special election, 1–2, 18–19, 139
spending, 5–6, 69–70, 95–96, 143, 146, 148–49

split districts, 108–9, 110–13, 119–20, 127–28, 150, 158
split tickets, 5–6, 17–18, 22, 25–26, 27–28, 38–39, 43–44, 70–71, 84, 92, 108–11, 127–28, 150–51, 158
straight tickets, 2, 17–18, 28, 39, 43–44, 87–88, 159
survey experiment, 10–11, 92, 117, 132–33, 159
Sweeney, Stephen, 155

Tea Party, 95–96
television, 68, 69–70
Texas, 64–65, 153–54
Theil, Peter, 20
thermometer ratings, 118–23
Trump, Donald 2, 7–8, 19–21, 64–65, 114, 118–19, 126–28, 129–31, 132–38, 140–41, 144–46, 147–50, 151–52, 153–54, 155–56, 161–64

Trump Jr., Donald, 20
Tuberville, Tommy, 140–41
turnout, 27, 139, 161
turnover, 58, 64, 68–69, 110, 112

valence, 117, 124–26
Vance, J.D., 20
Velde, Harold, 66
Virginia, 95–96, 144, 153–55
Vote Blue in 2022, 114
Vote Blue No Matter Who, 114
voter fraud. *See* election denialism
vote swing, 30–31, 101
Voting Rights Act, 66
vulnerability, 1, 44–45, 56, 57, 143

Webb, Cameron, 144

Youngkin, Glenn, 153–54

The manufacturer's authorised representative in the EU for product safety is Oxford
University Press España S.A. of El Parque Empresarial San Fernando de Henares,
Avenida de Castilla, 2 – 28830 Madrid (www.oup.es/en or product.safety@oup.com).
OUP España S.A. also acts as importer into Spain of products made by the manufacturer.

Printed in the USA/Agawam, MA
May 16, 2025

887590.005